GAME CHANGERS

YOU ARE GOD'S FIRST ROUND DRAFT CHOICE!

JAMES J. HOLDEN
FOUNDER, MANTOUR MINISTRIES

GAME CHANGERS

Copyright © 2025 Mantour Ministries

All rights reserved. No portion of this book may be reproduced, stored in a retrieval system, or transmitted in any form or by any means—electronic, mechanical, photocopy, recording, scanning, or other—except for brief quotations in reviews or articles without the prior written permission of the author.

Published by 4One Ministries, Inc. Visit www.mantourministries.com for more information on bulk discounts and special promotions, or e-mail your questions to info@4oneministries.org.

Workbook: OpenAI. ChatGPT (GPT-5). 2025. OpenAI, https://chat.openai.com/.

All Scripture quotations, unless otherwise indicated, are taken from the The ESV® Bible (The Holy Bible, English Standard Version®). ESV® Text Edition: 2016. Copyright © 2001 by Crossway, a publishing ministry of Good News Publishers.

The Holy Bible, New International Version®, NIV®. Copyright ©1973, 1978, 1984, 2011 by Biblica, Inc.™ Used by permission of Zondervan. All rights reserved worldwide. www.zondervan.com The "NIV" and "New International Version" are trademarks registered in the United States Patent and Trademark Office by Biblica, Inc.™

Scripture taken from the New King James Version®. Copyright © 1982 by Thomas Nelson. Used by permission. All rights reserved.

Scripture quotations marked (NLT) are taken from the Holy Bible, New Living Translation, copyright © 1996, 2004, 2007 by Tyndale House Foundation. Used by permission of Tyndale House Publishers, Inc., Carol Stream, Illinois 60188. All Scripture taken from the New Century Version®. Copyright © 2005 by Thomas Nelson. Used by permission. All rights reserved.

Design: James J. Holden

Subject Headings:
1. Christian life 2. Men's Ministry 3. Spiritual Growth

ISBN: 978-1-965809-06-8

Printed in the United States of America

DEDICATION

I want to dedicate this book to Bo Nix. It's not because he has revived the Denver Broncos with hope and energy, but because of the man he is on and off the field. Bo is a passionate believer who lives his faith. Reports say that during his interview with the Broncos before the draft, Coach Payton asked him to empty his backpack at the end, as no one seemed as perfect as Bo. Inside were notes on the playbook, pencils, and his Bible. Coach Payton knew at that moment he was the guy he wanted to draft!

Bo shines brightly everywhere. Bo has gained recognition for his commitment to not swearing—ever. He inspires his team while maintaining clean language. He consistently stands for God whenever possible. He is a Game-Changing man, and I dedicate this book to him.

TABLE OF CONTENTS

1. DRAFT DAY — 7
2. THE ONLY OPINION THAT MATTERS — 13
3. LIVING WITHOUT COMPROMISE IN A WORLD THAT CHEATS — 29
4. BUILDING WOMEN, NOT BARRIERS — 47
5. PROVE ME WRONG — 57
6. THE MAN BEHIND THE MAN — 73
7. ATAH HA'ISH'ING AUTHORITY — 85
8. A GREAT BIG WEE LITTLE MAN — 99
9. THE UNKNOWN MVP'S — 113
10. BLITZED FROM WITHIN — 121
11. CHAMPIONS DON'T PLAY ALONE — 133
12. BUILDING A DYNASTY — 145

WORKBOOK — 153

BIBLIOGRAPHY — 201

CHAPTER ONE
DRAFT DAY

Every year, the NFL Draft captures our attention. The cameras roll. The lights blaze. Analysts fill the air with speculation and endless debate. Fans gather around TVs, excitedly waiting to hear a name that could change the trajectory of their team. For a brief moment, hope floods in. Maybe this year will be different. This could be the player who can turn everything around.

For the athletes waiting to hear their names called, it's a night filled with nerves and anticipation. Hours of preparation, years of sweat, sacrifice, and grind have led to this moment. Young men sit with their families—hands clasped, wondering if their dream is about to come true. Will their name be called? Will a team see enough value in them to bring them on board, to believe in their potential, to build something around them?

It's a high-stakes moment. Everything feels like it hinges on that call.

But as powerful as the NFL Draft is, it's nothing compared to another draft that already happened. Before any commissioner ever stepped up to a podium, before any front office made their draft board, before any scout timed a 40-yard dash…God had already made His picks.

And here's the stunning truth: God chose you.

He didn't choose you because you could put up impressive stats. He didn't need to see your resume, your GPA, or your bank account. He wasn't waiting to find out if you could impress enough people or prove yourself to the world. God chose you before you even knew there was a game to play.

He chose you not because you were the fastest, the strongest, or the smartest, but because He loves you. He sees something in you that maybe you've never even seen in yourself. He knows the purpose He knit into your life. He knows the mission He designed that only you can do.

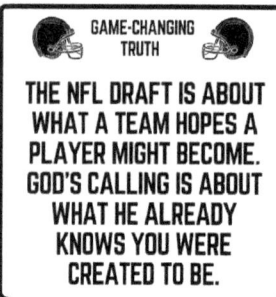

The NFL Draft is about what a team hopes a player might become.

God's calling is about what He already knows you were created to be.

That changes everything. Because when God calls you, it's not about trying to live up to a future you might or might not reach. It's about stepping into the calling He has already secured for you.

And here's another key difference: in the NFL, not everyone gets drafted. Thousands of players train, prepare, and dream, but only a few hundred will ever hear their names called. In God's Kingdom, everyone has a calling.

Jesus said in John 15:16, *"You did not choose me, but I chose you and appointed you that you should go and bear fruit."* (ESV)

He's not just filling a roster—He's raising up men who will change the game for eternity.

You've been drafted into a kingdom that desperately needs game-changing men. Men who will lead their families with love. Men who will stand firm in integrity when the culture bends and breaks. Men who will speak life to the broken, hope to the hopeless, and truth in a world full of lies. Men who will courageously follow Christ, even when compromise seems easier.

And make no mistake—you're not sitting on the bench. You're not stuck on the practice squad, waiting for a chance that may never come. No, you're already on the field. God has called you into the action of real life, with real stakes and eternal consequences.

You're not a backup plan. You're not an afterthought. You are a key player in God's divine strategy.

GAME-CHANGING TRUTH

YOU'RE NOT A BACKUP PLAN. YOU'RE NOT AN AFTERTHOUGHT. YOU ARE A KEY PLAYER IN GOD'S DIVINE STRATEGY.

So stop doubting your place. Stop wondering if you're worthy. Stop believing the lie that you don't matter. The God of the universe has called your name.

You've been chosen.

You've been appointed.

It's time to suit up and walk worthy of the One Who picked you.

Because this is more than a draft.

This is the call of a lifetime.

God has called you to be a game changer!

The Most Game-Changing Decision You'll Ever Make

Being chosen by God is incredible—but there's one decision that changes everything: choosing to respond to His call by accepting Jesus Christ as your Savior.

No career milestone, no championship, no earthly success will ever compare to the moment you step into a relationship with Jesus. That's the ultimate *"draft day"* moment…when you go from being lost to being found, from death to life, from living for yourself to living for God's Kingdom.

Romans 10:9 says, ***"If you confess with your mouth that Jesus is Lord and believe in your heart that God raised him from the dead, you will be saved."*** *(ESV)*

This isn't about earning a spot on God's team; it's about receiving the free gift Jesus paid for on the cross.

If you've never made that decision, this is your moment. You can make the most game-changing decision of your life right now, right where you are.

Heavenly Father,

I come to You in the name of Jesus, seeking Your forgiveness and grace. I acknowledge that I have sinned and fallen short of Your glory. I believe that Jesus Christ, Your Son, died on the cross for my sins and rose again, offering me the gift of eternal life.

Today, I turn from my old ways and ask You to cleanse my heart. I invite Jesus to come into my life, to be my Lord and Savior. I surrender my will to Yours, trusting in Your love and mercy.

Fill me with Your Holy Spirit, and help me to walk in Your truth and righteousness. Thank You for saving me, for making me a new creation in Christ.

In Jesus' name, I pray. Amen.

If you prayed that prayer, congratulations! That's your draft moment into God's kingdom. You are now a child of God, forgiven, and given a new identity in Christ. This book will help you take your first steps as a game-changing man of God.

As we move forward, I need you to understand this: **this book is not about football. It's about you—and the man God is calling you to become.** This world is in desperate need of men who will rise above the noise, take a stand for truth, and live with conviction. Men who are fully surrendered to God, grounded in His Word, and unwavering in their faith. Men who will stare down the evil in this world and, with courage and resolve, declare, *"I will do it God's way."*

In this book, we will look at past game-changers in God's kingdom. As we study their tape, we will glean from their stories what we can to become all that God has drafted us to be.

Each chapter will include group study questions, allowing you to work through them with a group of men. I STRONGLY encourage you to do this. We have been blown away by the testimonies of how God has worked through these books as men worked through them together in their men's ministry. There is strength in numbers. Work together with other men and choose to ride or die together.

The book also includes a workbook, allowing you to delve more deeply personally and providing a format for discussion in your small group.

GAME CHANGERS

Are you ready to put on the pads and be the game-changer God drafted you to be? Are you motivated to reach your full potential as a man of God and do the calling only you can do? If so, let's get started!

Dear Heavenly Father,

Thank You for choosing me before I ever knew You. Thank You for calling my name, for seeing purpose in me when I didn't see it myself. Help me to live like a man who has been drafted into Your Kingdom—with courage, integrity, and love. Teach me to walk worthy of Your calling and to bear fruit that will last. In Jesus' name, amen.

GROUP STUDY QUESTIONS

1. When you hear that God has chosen you, what emotions rise up—excitement, doubt, unworthiness, or gratitude? Why?

2. What lies have you believed about your value that God's truth in John 15:16 confronts?

3. In what areas of your life do you need to start living like you're *"on the field"* instead of sitting on the bench?

4. Who in your life needs to be reminded that they, too, have been chosen by God? How can you encourage them this week?

5. After reading this chapter, what is one thing you will put into practice or one thing you will change in your life?

6. How can we, as a group, help you do this?

CHAPTER TWO
THE ONLY OPINION THAT MATTERS

Before every NFL Draft, teams go through an extensive process to evaluate players. They watch countless hours of game tape, interview coaches, doctors, and even support staff to see how a player treats everyone around them. They hold workouts and ask tough, probing questions. After conducting this extensive research, they create a prospect report that outlines the strengths, weaknesses, and potential for success. It's almost a science. But even with all that analysis, teams sometimes get it completely wrong. For instance, take a look at this prospect report one team compiled on a defensive lineman.

"*Personnel director IV: The Gabe Carimi of defense. Not an elite athlete. A little stiff and on the ground too much. But he's system-friendly. Can rush inside or out.*

Personnel director V: Sharp kid, but not a football player. Those Wisconsin kids don't show up on tape.

Defensive coordinator II: I wanted to like him more than I did.

Head coach: Scares me. Not exceptional at anything. If you're not explosive and lack great quickness, you get locked up with those offensive tackles in this league and don't go anywhere."[1]

Summary: *"He won't ever be a stud pass rusher."*[1]

They really didn't like this player very much! Who was this player?

J.J. Watt, one of the greatest defensive players in NFL history.

Watt was a three-time NFL Defensive Player of the Year, made five Pro Bowls, was a five-time first-team All-Pro, and was the Walter Payton NFL Man of the Year in 2017. Those were some harsh words spoken about Watt. Thankfully, he ignored them and went on to become one of the greatest defensive linemen in history.

Many NFL players have faced similar criticism, with legendary figures like Bobby Wagner, Richard Seymour, Drew Brees, and Russell Wilson also receiving negative comments.

Many players might be hurt by negative comments. However, a game-changing player uses such comments as motivation to improve and prove others wrong. As men of God, we should follow this example.

I have seen way too many of God's sons become crippled and defeated by words spoken over them in life.

- *"You're worthless."*
- *"You'll never amount to anything."*
- *"You're too stupid."*
- *"You're weak."*
- *"You're a failure."*

- *"You'll never be good enough."*
- *"You're a mistake."*
- *"You're a loser."*
- *"Nobody will ever love you."*
- *"You're not tough enough."*
- *"You're a disappointment."*

Parents, teachers, friends, and relatives speak words into our lives that cut deep. They wound us, and too often, we carry their lies as truth. It's time for men of God to stop believing those lies and start living in the reality of how God sees them. We can break free from these lies and thoughts deep within us and instead overcome, becoming a game-changing man.

One of my favorite men in the Bible proves this point for us. Let's look at the life of David.

David is one of the most popular men in the Bible. He is mainly remembered for killing Goliath and being Israel's greatest king. Many know him as *"A man after God's own heart."* What a title. I don't know about you, but I would love for that to be my legacy. David was one of the most godly men who ever lived.

We first read about David in 1 Samuel 16:5-11 when God sent the prophet Samuel to Jesse's house to anoint the next king of Israel after Saul lost God's favor.

> ***He (Samuel) consecrated Jesse and his sons and invited them to the sacrifice.***
>
> ***When they came, he looked on Eliab and thought, "Surely the Lord's anointed is before him." But the Lord said to Samuel, "Do not look on his appearance or***

on the height of his stature, because I have rejected him. For the Lord sees not as man sees: man looks on the outward appearance, but the Lord looks on the heart." Then Jesse called Abinadab and made him pass before Samuel. And he said, "Neither has the Lord chosen this one." Then Jesse made Shammah pass by. And he said, "Neither has the Lord chosen this one." And Jesse made seven of his sons pass before Samuel. And Samuel said to Jesse, "The Lord has not chosen these." Then Samuel said to Jesse, "Are all your sons here?" And he said, "There remains yet the youngest, but behold, he is keeping the sheep." (ESV)

Do you believe it? Jesse thought so little of David that he didn't even invite him to the family reunion. He felt there was no way God would ever want David. All he felt David was good for was being a shepherd.

In today's day and age, being a shepherd is not a bad thing. However, in David's time, there was no worse profession for a Jew. Shepherds were ceremonially unclean. They were not permitted to enter the temple area to worship. They were unacceptable. They were nobodies. They could not be called as witnesses in court, for somebody had written that no one could believe the testimony of a shepherd. They were despised. They were looked down upon and often hated.

Shepherds were considered the least of all men. Jesse thought David was capable of no better. His family saw him as worthless.

As we move forward in David's life, we reach a pivotal point. Israel is in a fierce standoff with the Philistines. However, the Philistines have something the Israelites don't: a giant named Goliath. He was an unbeatable warrior…and he knew it. Every day, he took to the battlefield to taunt and humiliate the Israelite army.

David was called in from the field by his father and sent on an errand to deliver food to his brothers, who were serving in the army. David arrived on the scene just as Goliath began his daily intimidation routine. However, instead of cowering like the rest of the men, David got angry! How dare this giant attack David's God!

> *David said to the men who stood by him, ... who is this uncircumcised Philistine, that he should defy the armies of the living God? -1 Samuel 17:26 (ESV)*

David wasn't having it! Action had to be taken. But instead of being encouraged, he faced more insults and harsh words.

> *Now Eliab his eldest brother heard when he spoke to the men. And Eliab's anger was kindled against David, and he said, "Why have you come down? And with whom have you left those few sheep in the wilderness? I know your presumption and the evil of your heart, for you have come down to see the battle." -1 Samuel 17:28 (ESV)*

David didn't let these negative words stop him. He volunteered to fight Goliath.

> *He (David) took his staff in his hand and chose five smooth stones from the brook and put them in his shepherd's pouch. His sling was in his hand, and he approached the Philistine.*

> *And the Philistine moved forward and came near to David, with his shield-bearer in front of him. And when the Philistine looked and saw David, he disdained him, for he was but a youth, ruddy and handsome in appearance. And the Philistine said to David, "Am I a dog, that you come to me with sticks?" And the Philistine cursed David by his gods. The Philistine said to David, "Come to me, and I will*

> *give your flesh to the birds of the air and to the beasts of the field."*
>
> *Then David said to the Philistine, "You come to me with a sword and with a spear and with a javelin, but I come to you in the name of the Lord of hosts, the God of the armies of Israel, whom you have defied. This day the Lord will deliver you into my hand, and I will strike you down and cut off your head. And I will give the dead bodies of the host of the Philistines this day to the birds of the air and to the wild beasts of the earth, that all the earth may know that there is a God in Israel, and that all this assembly may know that the Lord saves not with sword and spear. For the battle is the Lord's, and he will give you into our hand." -1 Samuel 17:40-47 (ESV)*

Wow! Can David ever talk smack! But his smack was based on trust and belief in his God! He didn't believe the lies and cruel words spoken over him. His confidence and strength came from what God spoke into His life!

David's faith and belief in God paid off.

> *When the Philistine arose and came and drew near to meet David, David ran quickly toward the battle line to meet the Philistine. And David put his hand in his bag and took out a stone and slung it and struck the Philistine on his forehead. The stone sank into his forehead, and he fell on his face to the ground.*
>
> *So David prevailed over the Philistine with a sling and with a stone, and struck the Philistine and killed him. -1 Samuel 17:48-50 (ESV)*

God used David to defeat Goliath, making him a hero and a member of King Saul's court, where he was trusted and loved, especially by Jonathan, who became his mentor and friend. However, before long, Saul became jealous of David. Saul tried to kill him twice, forcing David to flee and leave his home and friends behind.

On the run, David faced harsh words from others, but he remembered God's promise that he would be king. He gathered fellow outcasts, formed a loyal army, and for a time, found acceptance. However, he was eventually worn down by harsh words that deeply affected him.

While hiding from Saul, David protected the shepherds and flocks of a wealthy man named Nabal. Later, he asked Nabal for food, expecting kindness, but he found the opposite.

> *Now Samuel died. And all Israel assembled and mourned for him, and they buried him in his house at Ramah.*
>
> *Then David rose and went down to the wilderness of Paran. And there was a man in Maon whose business was in Carmel. The man was very rich; he had three thousand sheep and a thousand goats. He was shearing his sheep in Carmel. Now the name of the man was Nabal, and the name of his wife Abigail. The woman was discerning and beautiful, but the man was harsh and badly behaved; he was a Calebite. -1 Samuel 25:1-3 (ESV)*

David was not in a good place. All the priests in Nob had been killed because of him (1 Samuel 22), and he was constantly on the run. Even after sparing Saul's life twice, Saul still hunted him. He sought refuge with the Philistines, who wanted him dead, forcing David to feign insanity to survive. (1 Samuel 21:10-15) Saul took his wife and gave her to another man. (1 Samuel 25:44) The man who had anointed him as future king had just died. (1 Samuel 25:1)

Perhaps David wondered if God's promise had died with him. He definitely was in mourning.

And he was hungry! He trusted that Nabal would repay him and his men for their protection, but Nabal proved to be a selfish, harsh man. Look at how he responded to David's men when they asked for food.

> *And Nabal answered David's servants, "Who is David? Who is the son of Jesse? There are many servants these days who are breaking away from their masters. Shall I take my bread and my water and my meat that I have killed for my shearers and give it to men who come from I do not know where?" So David's young men turned away and came back and told him all this. And David said to his men, "Every man strap on his sword!" -1 Samuel 25:10-13 (ESV)*

David went from hungry to hangry! He has had enough! He has been harassed and ridiculed for the last time! Nabal ridiculed David as a nobody who was no good. He put down his reputation, his lineage, and his name. Nabal would pay for his words with his life.

David has lost focus on what God thought of him and what God had promised him. He instead listened to words spoken to him by others, words he had endured his whole life. He strapped on his sword and went on a mission to kill Nabal and all of his family!

As we return to the passage, Abigail learns about Nabal's harsh words to David and David's anger. She quickly goes to him, apologizing for her husband, saying he is a jerk, and everyone knows it. But she doesn't want to see David destroy himself because of her husband. She then speaks the words that David needs to remember.

> *Please forgive the trespass of your servant. For the Lord will certainly make my lord a sure house, because*

my lord is fighting the battles of the Lord, and evil shall not be found in you so long as you live. If men rise up to pursue you and to seek your life, the life of my lord shall be bound in the bundle of the living in the care of the Lord your God. And the lives of your enemies he shall sling out as from the hollow of a sling.

And when the Lord has done to my lord according to all the good that he has spoken concerning you and has appointed you prince over Israel, my lord shall have no cause of grief or pangs of conscience for having shed blood without cause or for my lord working salvation himself.
-1 Samuel 25:28-31 (ESV)

Abigail reminded David that he already had God's acceptance. It didn't matter what her husband thought, what his father said, or even that Saul wanted him dead—God had chosen David. No insult could diminish him, no enemy could destroy him, because God Himself had called him His own. David was loved, accepted, and protected by God, and all his needs could be met by God alone.

We need to hear these same truths: Our worth isn't based on what others say about us. It's based on God's unchanging Word. People can say things that hurt, discourage, or belittle us. Family might ignore us, leaders might dismiss us, and enemies might come against us. But none of those voices is the final truth. Only God's Word is.

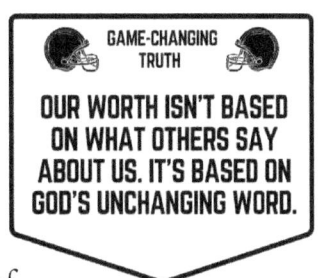

GAME-CHANGING TRUTH

OUR WORTH ISN'T BASED ON WHAT OTHERS SAY ABOUT US. IT'S BASED ON GOD'S UNCHANGING WORD.

When God calls us His children, that can't be taken away. When He says we're forgiven, no accusation can condemn us. When He says we are chosen, loved, and holy, no insult or rejection can change that. His Word is powerful, eternal, and greater than any opinion about us.

Just as David did, we'll face times when people mock us, doubt us, or threaten us. But we can remember that God has spoken a greater word—that He is for us, His plans are good, and His promises will never fail.

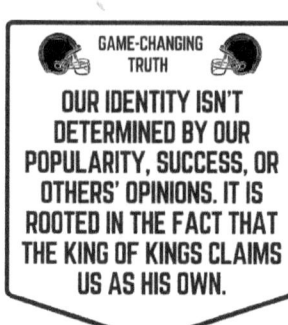

GAME-CHANGING TRUTH

OUR IDENTITY ISN'T DETERMINED BY OUR POPULARITY, SUCCESS, OR OTHERS' OPINIONS. IT IS ROOTED IN THE FACT THAT THE KING OF KINGS CLAIMS US AS HIS OWN.

Our identity isn't determined by our popularity, success, or others' opinions. It is rooted in the fact that the King of Kings claims us as His own. When we rely on God's truth, we can stand firm against any opposition.

Game-changing men must know and believe this deep inside. We need to use God's Word to counter the lies spoken against us.

- People may say: *"You're worthless."* But the Bible says: ***"You are fearfully and wonderfully made." (Psalm 139:14, ESV)***

- People may say: *"You'll never amount to anything."* But the Bible says: ***"For I know the plans I have for you... plans to prosper you and not to harm you." (Jeremiah 29:11, NIV)***

- People may say: *"You're too stupid to get it right."* But the Bible says: ***"If any of you lacks wisdom, let him ask God... and it will be given to him." (James 1:5, ESV)***

- People may say: *"You're weak."* But the Bible says: ***"My grace is sufficient for you, for my power is made perfect in weakness." (2 Corinthians 12:9, ESV)***

- People may say: *"You're a failure."* But the Bible says: ***"In all these things we are more than conquerors through him who loved us." (Romans 8:37, ESV)***

- People may say: *"You'll never be good enough."* But the Bible says: ***"There is therefore now no condemnation for those who are in Christ Jesus." (Romans 8:1, ESV)***

- People may say: *"You're a mistake."* But the Bible says: ***"Before I formed you in the womb I knew you." (Jeremiah 1:5, ESV)***

- People may say: *"You're a loser."* But the Bible says: ***"Thanks be to God, who gives us the victory through our Lord Jesus Christ." (1 Corinthians 15:57, ESV)***

- People may say: *"Nobody will ever love you."* But the Bible says: ***"We love because He first loved us." (1 John 4:19, ESV)***

- People may say: *"You're not tough enough."* But the Bible says: ***"Be strong and courageous. Do not be frightened, and do not be dismayed, for the Lord your God is with you wherever you go." (Joshua 1:9, ESV)***

- People may say: *"You're a disappointment."* But the Bible says: ***"See what kind of love the Father has given to us, that we should be called children of God." (1 John 3:1, ESV)***

Like David, we must reject the lies spoken over us. At the same time, we can't ignore the effect these words had on us. We need to be honest about the ways those words have shaped us, the pain they created, the choices we made in response, and the consequences that followed. We can't ignore the wounds, but we can face them and let the Holy Spirit heal what's been broken.

God will replace every lie with truth. He reminds us that we are not weak, worthless, or defeated…we are His beloved children, chosen, strong, and empowered to live out the unique purpose He designed for us.

David was able to conquer the pain caused by Nabals' words and move forward as a man who didn't let others' words affect him. How do I know this? We see it in the Bible.

In 2 Samuel 16, David, now the king (as God had promised), is fleeing for his life from his son Absalom, who is attempting to seize the throne. As he and his men leave the city, a man named Shimei comes out, cursing David and throwing stones at him.

> *And Shimei said as he cursed, "Get out, get out, you man of blood, you worthless man! The Lord has avenged on you all the blood of the house of Saul, in whose place you have reigned, and the Lord has given the kingdom into the hand of your son Absalom. See, your evil is on you, for you are a man of blood." -2 Samuel 16:7-8 (ESV)*

Shimei's words and actions were harsh and insulting. David's men, including Abishai, wanted to kill him. But David refused. He recognized that God's purposes were greater than Shimei's curses. David said:

> *Leave him alone, and let him curse, for the Lord has told him to. It may be that the Lord will look on the wrong done to me, and that the Lord will repay me with good for his cursing today. -2 Samuel 16:11-12 (ESV)*

David didn't respond in anger. He trusted God's Word above the insults thrown at him, letting God handle what others tried to use to harm him. By doing this, he was able to rise above harsh words and trust in God's justice and timing. He now understood his true identity in God—his worth and esteem came from his relationship with the Lord, not from what Shimei or anyone else thought. David believed God loved him and would vindicate him, just as Abigail had reminded him years before.

Men, if you want to be a game-changing man, you must make a deliberate choice to reject the lies, insults, and harsh words spoken over you. The world will try to define you by your failures, your appearance, your past, or the opinions of others. However, God sees you differently. Who you are isn't defined by what others say, but by what God says about you. He is the One Who knows your heart, your purpose, and your potential.

Build your identity on what God says. Let His Word shape how you see yourself, guide your decisions, and fuel your courage. Spend time with Him every day —pray, read the Bible, think on His promises, and let His truth reset your mind. Invite Him to heal the places hurt by rejection, criticism, or failure. In His eyes, you are loved, chosen, strong, and equipped to live out the purpose He made you for.

> **GAME-CHANGING TRUTH**
> WHO YOU ARE ISN'T DEFINED BY WHAT OTHERS SAY, BUT BY WHAT GOD SAYS ABOUT YOU. HE IS THE ONE WHO KNOWS YOUR HEART, YOUR PURPOSE, AND YOUR POTENTIAL.

As a game-changing man, you've got to learn to rise above the criticism and attacks that come your way. Like David, you'll run into people who doubt you, talk against you, or try to drag you down. But God's Word tells a different story. Others may mock or threaten, but God is your defender. His promises are solid, and no one's words can stop His plan for your life.

David's story shows us that people's insults lose their power when we stand on the truth of God's Word. He didn't let Goliath's taunts, Nabal's disrespect, or Shimei's curses define him. He trusted God's voice above everything else, and that gave him courage and confidence. You can do the same. Stand firm, stay focused, and refuse to let criticism divert you from your path.

If their words don't line up with God's Word, it's a lie. Every insult or rejection is just another chance to remember what God says about you. Let His Word set your identity—not other people's opinions. Walk strong in His calling, knowing your strength and confidence come from the God Who made you, loves you, and will never leave you.

Just as David did, you can rise above the opinions of others. You can live with the power, courage, and confidence that come from understanding your identity in God. You can be a game-changing man who impacts the world—not because of your own strength or status, but because of your unwavering faith in God's Word. Claim this identity today, and let God's truth guide you, lead you, and empower you to fulfill your divine purpose.

Heavenly Father,

I come before You today acknowledging the lies and harsh words that have tried to define me. You see the wounds left by the voices of parents, teachers, friends, and enemies alike. Lord, I ask You to heal those wounds, restore my heart, and remind me of my true identity in You.

Help me, Father, to reject every lie spoken over me. Teach me to anchor my worth in Your Word, to stand firm in Your truth, and to trust Your promises above the opinions and insults of others. Like David, may I walk in courage, faith, and confidence, knowing that You are my defender, my refuge, and my provider.

Empower me, Lord, to become a game-changing man who impacts the world for Your glory. Let my life reflect Your love, my words bring encouragement, and my actions honor Your name. Protect me from bitterness, and help me rise above every attack, every insult, and every discouragement.

I thank You, Lord, that You see me, love me, and have called me chosen, strong, and empowered for Your purpose. May I live each day in the freedom and victory that comes from knowing who I am in You. In Jesus' name, Amen.

GROUP STUDY QUESTIONS:

1. What are some lies or harsh words you've believed about yourself in the past?

2. How do these compare to what God says about you in His Word?

3. How does basing your identity in God's Word change the way you handle criticism or rejection?

4. Which of God's promises resonates with you most when facing discouragement?

5. What steps can you take this week to reinforce your identity in God rather than in the approval of others?

6. How can you use your experiences of overcoming harsh words to encourage or mentor someone else?

7. After reading this chapter, what is one thing you will put into practice or one thing you will change in your life?

8. How can we, as a group, help you do this?

CHAPTER THREE
LIVING WITHOUT COMPROMISE IN A WORLD THAT CHEATS

I could hardly believe the text my sister had sent.

It was a link to an article about well-known Christian musician Michael Tait, accusing him of living a double life, using drugs, and making unwanted sexual advances toward men.

"Is this true?" I replied.

Sadly, it would only be a few days until Michael Tait would release a statement admitting that *"for years I (Michael) have lied and deceived my family, friends, fans, and even misled my bandmates about aspects of my life. I was, for the most part, living two distinctly different lives. I was not the same person on stage Sunday night that I was at home on Monday."*[1]

In his own words, he admitted that the accusations mainly were true—he had used alcohol, drank too much, and made unwanted sexual advances toward men for over two decades.

I must admit that, being a huge DC Talk fan growing up, this news hit me particularly hard. I felt shocked, stunned, angry, and disappointed to hear once again that a prominent Christian leader was saying one thing from the stage while hiding a sinful lifestyle.

Sadly, this list of names that fit this description is too long. It's no wonder that too many unbelievers have the same feelings as a popular television host who recently said, *"I find, unfortunately, in my life experience is that most people who put God in front of them were full of it and dangerous."* 2

What a sad statement! Here's the thing—this man wasn't being hateful when he said it. I watched the episode, and he was being vulnerable and honest.

Sadly, too many people have this same experience with the church and Christianity. The only thing that will change their hearts and minds is to encounter Christians who live differently. If we want to be game-changing men who change the narrative, one of the most significant character traits we need to possess is integrity.

Let's start by taking a look at what this word means.

Integrity is *the quality of being honest and having strong moral principles that you refuse to change. The quality of being honest and having strong moral principles.*3

A good Biblical example of this is found in the life of Joseph.

Even as I write that, I can hear you thinking, *"Okay, this is the chapter about sexual integrity."*

Well, yes, and no.

While Joseph's refusal to flee from Potiphar's wife in Genesis 39 is a notable example of his integrity, it is just one of the many ways he demonstrated it. Joseph didn't earn integrity in that one moment of temptation—he already had it. Integrity is what enabled him to resist. In this chapter, we will explore several more examples and discuss how we can follow his example to live as men of integrity in all aspects of our lives.

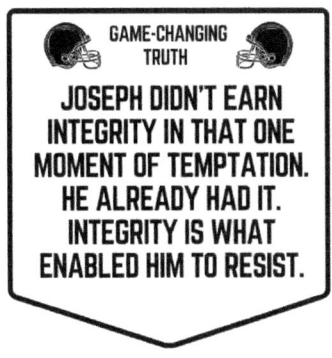

For those unfamiliar with Joseph, here's his background. He was born into a large, troubled family. His father, Jacob, struggled with honesty, using trickery to secure blessings—first deceiving Esau to give Joseph the family blessing (Genesis 27), which made Esau furious and forced Jacob to flee to his uncle Laban (Genesis 27:41-45).

Initially, Laban welcomed Jacob, put him in charge of his flocks, and agreed to let him marry Rachel after seven years of work. However, Laban, being a deceitful man himself, tricked Jacob on his wedding night by swapping Rachel for Leah, which led to a complicated family dynamic. By the time Joseph was born, tensions ran high due to Jacob's favoritism toward Rachel. Joseph became his father's favorite, especially after Rachel died giving birth to Benjamin, which fueled his brothers' jealousy and hatred even more.

This is where Joseph's story takes a pivotal and tragic turn:

> *Now his brothers had gone to graze their father's flocks near Shechem, and Israel said to Joseph, "As you know, your brothers are grazing the flocks near Shechem. Come, I am going to send you to them."…*

> *So Joseph went after his brothers and found them near Dothan. But they saw him in the distance, and before he reached them, they plotted to kill him.*
>
> *"Here comes that dreamer!" they said to each other. "Come now, let's kill him and throw him into one of these cisterns and say that a ferocious animal devoured him. Then we'll see what comes of his dreams." -Genesis 37:12, 17-20 (NIV)*

And that's what they did. At least until they saw some Midianite merchants come down the road, then, they had a better idea: we'll sell him and make a profit!

For twenty shekels of silver, Joseph was sold to the merchants who took him to Egypt and sold him to Potiphar, the captain of Pharaoh's guard.

What a tragic story! Here's a young man, just seventeen years old, who grew up in a seriously dysfunctional family, hated by his brothers, and sold as a slave to a man who was known for his cruelty and brutality. It seemed like his life was over. Yet, in God's plan, his life was beginning.

Here's the amazing part: despite all he went through, Joseph's reputation was not marked by anger, victimhood, or deceit following his father's footsteps. Instead, his story demonstrates resilience, integrity, and a profound commitment to God's laws. It reminds us that regardless of background or experiences, we can become men of integrity.

Let's look at some specific ways Joseph demonstrated integrity:

1. Joseph showed integrity in the workplace.

As we said earlier, Joseph was sold as a slave to Potiphar, who was the chief of the executioners, an elite force in Pharaoh's army. This was one tough dude Joseph now served! Think men like Vin Diesel or "The Rock" Dwayne Johnson. Joseph had to grow up fast to survive in this man's household.

However, Joseph did more than survive his job—he thrived in it. So much so that Potiphar took notice, and Joseph received a huge promotion.

> *Joseph found favor in his eyes and became his attendant. Potiphar put him in charge of his household, and he entrusted to his care everything he owned.*
>
> *From the time he put him in charge of his household and of all that he owned, the Lord blessed the household of the Egyptian because of Joseph. The blessing of the Lord was on everything Potiphar had, both in the house and in the field.*
>
> *So Potiphar left everything he had in Joseph's care; with Joseph in charge, he did not concern himself with anything except the food he ate. -Genesis 39:4-6 (NIV)*

Let's take a moment and think about this: Potiphar trusted Joseph completely, assigning him responsibility for his entire household. This included managing finances, overseeing the household budget, supervising other servants, and maintaining the property, house, and fields. Can you imagine how much Potiphar respected and trusted Joseph's integrity that he put a foreign slave in charge of everything?

Let's be honest: powerful men like Potiphar don't put just anyone in charge.

This promotion shows that Joseph was a hard worker. He had a good attitude. He was trustworthy, honest, and of the highest integrity. It was these qualities, combined with God's blessing, that made Joseph so successful that Potiphar noticed and promoted him.

It's important to notice that this didn't just happen at Potiphar's house.

Go to the end of the chapter and see that the same thing happened after Joseph was unfairly and unjustly put into prison.

> *So the warden put Joseph in charge of all those held in the prison, and he was made responsible for all that was done there. The warden paid no attention to anything under Joseph's care, because the Lord was with Joseph and gave him success in whatever he did. -Genesis 39:22-23 (NIV)*

Later, in Genesis 41, we see that after Joseph interpreted Pharaoh's dream, he was made second in command to Pharaoh. Rather than sitting in the lap of luxury and enjoying the promotion, Joseph went to work, creating and overseeing the plan that would provide the land of Egypt — and ultimately the surrounding world — with food during the famine.

Looking over Joseph's entire work history, we see that, whether in prison or the palace, he was a man of integrity.

His life challenges us to ask ourselves: *When it comes to our work, are we following his example? Is our integrity obvious to all?*

Think about it for a moment:

- Are you a hard worker?

- Do you clock in on time and give a hard day's work?

- Can your boss trust that when he gives you an assignment, it will be done well, without cutting corners or slacking off?

- Can you be trusted not to skim a little off the top, take a little from the cash register, or cook the books in your favor?

- Do you exhibit trustworthiness, responsibility, and honesty among your co-workers?

- Do you treat those who work under you fairly?

- As you go through your job day after day, do you exhibit integrity?

- If not, what do you need to change to follow Joseph's example and be a game-changing man of integrity?

Here's the thing—outside of our families, our jobs are the most significant part of our lives. It's where we spend most of our time and where we have the most influence. If we want to be game-changing men who demonstrate to the world what it truly means to be a man of God, we must exhibit integrity in the workplace. If Joseph could do it in each of his challenging situations, so can you.

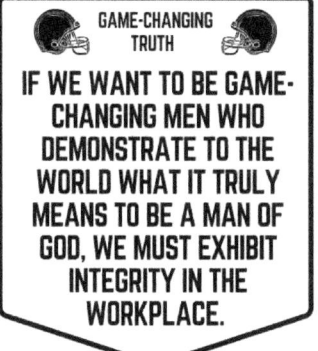

GAME-CHANGING TRUTH

IF WE WANT TO BE GAME-CHANGING MEN WHO DEMONSTRATE TO THE WORLD WHAT IT TRULY MEANS TO BE A MAN OF GOD, WE MUST EXHIBIT INTEGRITY IN THE WORKPLACE.

2. Joseph had sexual integrity.

"Ha! I knew you'd get there!"

Obviously, you can't talk about Joseph's integrity without talking about his encounter with Mrs. Potiphar.

Most of us know the story of Mrs. Potiphar taking notice of Joseph while he was a faithful worker in Potiphar's house.

> ***Now Joseph was well-built and handsome, and after a while his master's wife took notice of Joseph and said, "Come to bed with me!"*** *-Genesis 39:6-7 (NIV)*

So Joseph is finally starting to hit his stride. He's gone from slave to Potiphar's personal assistant. Things are finally looking up. That is, until Mrs. Potiphar got hot and bothered. Now Joseph has to deal with this!

Here's where Joseph's integrity shines: even though Mrs. Potiphar apparently propositioned him every day, Joseph turned her down.

> ***And though she spoke to Joseph day after day, he refused to go to bed with her or even be with her.*** *-Genesis 39:10 (NIV)*

Think about this for a moment.

Joseph is a young man—at the height of his sexual peak, his hormones are raging. He's in a strange land, has no family, no support system, and no one holding him accountable. Honestly, after what God allowed to happen to him, he would have every logical reason to be angry and choose to reject God's Laws and live a life of sin.

Along comes this woman who is most likely attractive. And every single day, she asks him to sleep with her.

Can you imagine the temptation?

Yet, Joseph resists the temptation because, as he says, *"How then could I do such a wicked thing and sin against God?" -Genesis 39:9 (NIV)*.

Guys, think about this for a moment. Joseph sets the standard for sexual integrity. Integrity isn't found in the escape; it's what gives you the courage to escape. If Joseph can stay faithful to God and resist temptation in these circumstances, what is our excuse?

Still, this is a particularly damaging area for men. Numerous stories exist of men who professed to follow Christ and lost their reputation because of a sex scandal. It's not limited to public figures; it occurs in churches and communities of all sizes across the nation.

What our world needs is game-changing men of God who, like Joseph, commit themselves to being men of sexual integrity.

- We need single and divorced men to commit themselves to abstinence before marriage—both physically, mentally, and virtually.
- Married men need to stop entertaining the idea of adultery—this includes physical and emotional adultery, or through online communications.
- It's time that the men of God did whatever it takes to overcome their addiction to pornography.
- Godly men need to be men who respect women and treat women as sisters in Christ rather than sexual objects.

Adopting the attitude of Joseph, we need to recognize that every sexual sin is a sin against God and become men of sexual integrity. When sexual temptation comes our way in any form, we need to follow Joseph's example and flee.

3. Joseph had integrity when he was a victim.

As we continue to read Genesis 39, we see that no one in Potiphar's palace stood up and cheered because Joseph was a man of sexual integrity. Instead, Mrs. Potiphar made up a lie and told her husband that Joseph had propositioned her.

Whether or not Potiphar believed his wife, the lie landed Joseph in jail for something he didn't do. Once again, Joseph was a victim.

Yet, Joseph didn't wallow in his victimhood, become angry with God, or give up his integrity. Instead, he continued being who he had always been, which allowed God to use him in prison. (Genesis 39:16-23)

Here's the thing: life isn't always fair. Too often, when we experience unjust treatment, our first response is to play the victim. We feel sorry for ourselves, and before long, we start excusing our sins. We begin believing lies like, *"I deserve to do this…look what happened to me,"* or *"What does it matter anyway, no matter what I do, I suffer. Why not enjoy myself?"*

Joseph remained faithful to God and maintained his integrity during his imprisonment, even serving so well that he was put in charge of the prison. This wouldn't have happened if he had played the victim or used his injustice as an excuse for sin.

It's the same for us. Just because God allows a detour, an injustice, or a hard time in our lives doesn't give us an excuse to fool around with sin. Instead, we need to walk CLOSER to God and lead a holier life because this is the attitude that opens the door for God to bless us and get us out of the situation.

While I can't promise a happy ending like Joseph's, I can guarantee that playing the victim, harboring bitterness, or compromising your integrity will cause you to miss the life God has planned for you. If you use being a victim as an excuse for sin, you'll just be another sad, lost soul among the many failed Christian men.

But it doesn't have to be that way. You can choose to mimic Joseph by saying, *"No matter what, I will maintain my integrity,"* becoming a strong example of a game-changing man of God.

4. Joseph demonstrated integrity while in power.

Thankfully, the prison was not the end of Joseph's story. After two years in prison, Joseph heard a knock on his cell door. Pharaoh had a dream no one could interpret. Remembering Joseph's gift, the cupbearer mentioned him. (Genesis 41) Within a day, Joseph went from prisoner to Egypt's second-in-command, overseeing food storage during abundance and distribution during famine for the next fourteen years.

Through it all, he maintained his integrity. He worked hard. He was diligent. He was honest. Ultimately, God used him to save Egypt and the surrounding areas.

Joseph now faced one of life's toughest tests: holding onto integrity in the face of power. It's easy to be honest, hardworking, and loyal in the pit, dreaming of a better life. But all too often, promotion, fame, or wealth corrupts, and people crumble under the weight of this power.

Joseph was different. He carried the same character from the pit into the palace, using his authority not for ego or control, but to serve, lead, and help others.

How do we know this?

Fast forward to Genesis 50. Jacob, Joseph's father, died. At the end of Genesis 50:3, it says, **"And the Egyptians mourned for him seventy days." (NIV)**

The Egyptian people weren't mourning for Jacob—he was just a nomadic shepherd with a big, messed-up family. They mourned for Joseph, a leader they loved. People don't grieve like this for oppressive, unjust, or dishonest leaders; they do it for someone they trust, love, and believe has helped them.

Today, the question we need to ask ourselves is: *when I am succeeding, when I have power (either a little or a lot), when things are going well, and I'm on top of the world, am I still living with integrity?*

Am I still working hard?

Am I still being honest, truthful, and living in accordance with God's Word?

It's a curious phenomenon; people in power often fall into the same traps as those in the pit. They believe the lie of *"I'm special"*, *"I deserve it,"* or *"the rules don't apply to me anymore."*

Yet, it is just these prideful attitudes that lead to a fall. (Proverbs 16:18)

If we want to be game-changing men of God, we must be mindful of the pitfalls of success and resolve to maintain our integrity, even in positions of power.

Now, let's wrap it up by looking at one last area where Joseph maintained his integrity. Perhaps it is the most difficult of all.

5. Joseph maintained his integrity in his personal relationships.

As we examine the life of Joseph, we see that he was a remarkable individual. One of the most amazing ways he demonstrated his integrity was when his brothers came to Egypt seeking food.

Right away, Joseph recognized them.

Let's be honest, after what they did to him, he had every reason to tell them to go home and starve. He could have said, *"How do you like me now? Now, what do you think of my dreams? Have fun chewing on rocks."* But he didn't.

Instead, after a series of character tests (to see who he was dealing with and whether they were trustworthy or deceivers, like their father), Joseph brought them all to Egypt. He sent them up to a nice place and provided for them and their entire families throughout the famine.

Let's be honest—that was pretty incredible considering they tried to kill him but settled on selling him. But then, in Genesis 50, we see Joseph's integrity shine yet again.

Jacob has died, and the funeral is over.

Joseph's brothers start thinking, *"What if he was only kind to us because he loved Dad?"* (A legit thought after what they did.)

So they once again connive a plan and send a message to Joseph saying, *"Jacob left a message saying you should forgive your brothers for what they did and not punish them."*

Here's where we see Joseph's integrity shine brighter than ever before.

> ***When their message came to him, Joseph wept.***
>
> ***His brothers then came and threw themselves down before him. "We are your slaves," they said.***
>
> ***But Joseph said to them, "Don't be afraid. Am I in the place of God? You intended to harm me, but God intended it for good to accomplish what is now being done, the saving of many lives.***
>
> ***So then, don't be afraid. I will provide for you and your children." And he reassured them and spoke kindly to them.***
> ***-Genesis 50:17-21 (NIV)***

He could have taken revenge. They certainly deserved it.

He could have had them killed or imprisoned.

He could have thrown them out of Egypt. He could have said, "Brother Benjamin, you and your family can stay, but the rest of you are on your own. I'm done."

But he didn't.

Instead, he forgave them. He continued to walk in his integrity, treat them better than they deserved to be treated, and take care of his family. His example sets the benchmark for what it means to be a game-changing man of God.

It means loving your enemies, even when they don't deserve it, being the bigger person, and choosing forgiveness when vengeance is easier. Being a game-changing man of God means taking care of your family, being responsible, and doing all that you can to heal personal relationships.

As we wrap up our examination of Joseph's integrity, one final question we must ask ourselves is: *"Am I walking in integrity in my personal relationships?"*

- Am I being honest with my wife and children?
- Am I consistently acting toward my family as Jesus would?
- When someone hurts me, do I seek revenge or forgiveness?
- Am I willing to restore broken relationships?

Let's be real—this isn't always easy, especially when relationships are broken, like in a divorce. Yet even in life's toughest moments, God calls His men to integrity in every relationship. We are called to choose peace over anger and conflict, to be peacemakers who seek not only our own good but the good of others, and to bring healing to difficult situations.

The reality is that every situation is unique, making it hard to give exact rules or advice. I have relationships in my own life that are complicated, yet I strive to handle them with integrity, grace, and love, even when they're far from perfect. I may not be able to give you all the specifics, but I can challenge you to choose integrity in every relationship. Follow Joseph's example, and let everyone in your life know you are doing your best to follow Jesus.

The truth is that Joseph was a fantastic man. He was a game-changer in his world, and by following his example, you can do the same in yours.

Today, you might be asking, *"How? How did he live with such integrity?"*

Joseph tells us throughout his story that he saw everything in his life through the lens of his relationship with God.

Remember, he told Potiphar's wife, he couldn't sin against God. (Genesis 39:9)

He told Pharaoh that it was not he, but God, who could interpret dreams. (Genesis 41:16)

He told his brothers that what they meant for evil, God meant for good. (Genesis 50:20)

Joseph could maintain his integrity because he maintained his personal relationship with God. He was deeply invested in pleasing God and living for Him. If we want to be like Joseph, we also need to put God first and live our lives for Him.

In all that we do, we need to: **Work heartily, as for the Lord and not for men, knowing that from the Lord you will receive the inheritance as your reward. You are serving the Lord Christ. -Colossians 3:23-24 ESV**

In our work, we must, **Serve wholeheartedly, as if you were serving the Lord, not people. -Ephesians 6:7 (NIV)**

In every part of our lives, we should strive to obey this verse: **Keep your conscience clear. Then if people speak against you, they will be ashamed when they see what a good life you live because you belong to Christ. -1 Peter 3:16 (NLT)**

Fixing our eyes on Jesus and relying on Him, we can follow Joseph's example and be game-changing men of integrity.

Heavenly Father,

Thank You for Joseph's example of integrity in every season—hardship, temptation, and power. Forgive me for the times I've compromised or let sin take root. Fill me with Your Spirit—give me courage, wisdom, and strength to stand for truth, lead justly, and resist temptation.

Help me forgive, restore, and love even when it's hard. May my life reflect Your goodness, walking in integrity and serving wholeheartedly as if serving Christ. Keep my heart focused on You, so all I do honors and glorifies Your name. In Jesus' name, Amen.

GROUP STUDY QUESTIONS:

1. How do you define integrity in your own words?

2. What lessons can we learn from Joseph about the importance of working hard, being trustworthy, and leading by example?

3. Are there temptations at work (cutting corners, dishonesty, gossip) that challenge your integrity? How can you address them?

4. How do you guard your own heart, mind, and actions against sexual temptation in daily life? What accountability steps or strategies can help you maintain sexual integrity?

5. When you experience injustice, unfair treatment, or betrayal, what are your natural responses?

6. How do you think power or success could test your integrity today? What practical steps can you take to stay humble and faithful when given more responsibility or influence?

7. What does it look like for you to live out integrity in family, friendships, or your community?

8. Which area of integrity—work, sexual, in injustice, in power, or in relationships—feels most challenging for you right now?

9. What one action can you take this week to grow in integrity?

10. How can we, as a group, help you with this?

CHAPTER FOUR
BUILDING WOMEN, NOT BARRIERS

I love a good quote! I have a list of quotes on my phone that I am constantly adding to. When I hear some amazing words spoken or read something that contains timeless wisdom, I pull out my phone and jot it down on my list. Here is a sample of some of my favorites.

- *"Those who say it can't be done, would you just please stop interrupting those of us that are doing it?"* -Dolly Parton, *Christmas at Dollywood*[1]

- *"Only when I cease to breathe will I be dead"* (it's funny). -Haru, *Beverly Hills Ninja*[2]

- *"The thing about decisions is you never have to talk yourself into the right ones."* -Commissioner Frank Reagan, *Blue Bloods*[3]

- *"Never get comfortable with making the Holy Spirit uncomfortable."* -Scott Kramer

- *"The dash on your tombstone is your life. Make the dash mean something."* -Mike Heck, *The Middle*[4]

- "Waste no more time arguing what a good man should be. Be one." -Marcus Aurelius[5]

- "You don't do business with crooks. Once they lie to you about one thing, they are going to lie to you about something else." -Dave Ramsey[6]

- "Listen, it's too big a world to be in competition with everybody else. The only guy I have to get better than is who I am right now." -Colonel Sherman T. Potter, *M.A.S.H.*[7]

The Bible also has many great quotes. In this chapter, we will examine one of my favorites, spoken by an amazing, game-changing man of God, Mordecai.

> **"And who knows whether you have not come to the kingdom for such a time as this?" -Esther 4:14 (ESV)**

Here's an interesting fact about this quote: when most of us hear it, our minds immediately go to Queen Esther. It's often regarded as a *"women's quote"* and frequently used at women's conferences.

But here's the thing…this quote was actually said by a game-changing man, Mordecai, encouraging a woman in his family to step into her God-given calling and responsibility.

For those not familiar with the story of Mordecai and Esther, let's recap. Mordecai was a Jew living as an exile in Persia. Esther 2 tells us that his father was one of the captives taken away from Jerusalem by Nebuchadnezzar. Mordecai was born and raised in captivity, but he was still fiercely loyal to his Jewish faith. Other than that dedication, there doesn't seem to be anything exceptional about him. He's just a godly man living his life.

Until there's a tragedy in his family. At some point, his uncle died and left behind an orphan daughter, Esther. Being a good man, Mordecai took her into his home and raised her as his own.

As we read the book of Esther, we see that King Ahasuerus threw a party where he and his guests got ridiculously drunk, and as often happens when intoxicated, he made some terrible decisions, resulting in him banishing his wife, Queen Vashti, from his presence forever. However, he eventually sobered up and realized how stupid he had been and that he needed a queen in his life.

He made a decree that made every beautiful girl in his city part of his harem. Each girl was presented to the king until he found one that pleased him. Unfortunately, Esther was a very beautiful girl. She was chosen to become a part of the king's harem.

This must have broken Mordecai's heart. As the king's gatekeeper, he knew the horrors these girls experienced. Now his little girl, his adopted daughter, was to become one of them. Not only that, but she was not a Persian. She was a Jew. Mordecai didn't want her pointing out this fact for her safety.

> ***Esther had not made known her people or kindred, for Mordecai had commanded her not to make it known. And every day Mordecai walked in front of the court of the harem to learn how Esther was and what was happening to her. -Esther 2:10-11 (ESV)***

Daily, Mordecai would go and check on Esther. He made sure she was okay. He gave her counsel and instruction on how to handle her new life. He never stopped taking care of her and being concerned for her.

Eventually, her night with the king came. The king chose her to be his new queen. Even after this new development, Mordecai continued to watch over her, advise her, and support her in her new role.

Then came the day that Mordecai heard the horrific news. Thanks to the evil Haman, a date was set for all Jews throughout the kingdom of Ahasuerus to be destroyed. Mordecai's first reaction was to put on sackcloth and ashes and cry out in a loud voice. This didn't go unnoticed by Esther.

> *When Esther's young women and her eunuchs came and told her, the queen was deeply distressed. She sent garments to clothe Mordecai, so that he might take off his sackcloth, but he would not accept them. Then Esther called for Hathach, one of the king's eunuchs, who had been appointed to attend her, and ordered him to go to Mordecai to learn what this was and why it was.*
>
> *Hathach went out to Mordecai in the open square of the city in front of the king's gate, and Mordecai told him all that had happened to him, and the exact sum of money that Haman had promised to pay into the king's treasuries for the destruction of the Jews. Mordecai also gave him a copy of the written decree issued in Susa for their destruction, that he might show it to Esther and explain it to her and command her to go to the king to beg his favor and plead with him on behalf of her people. -Esther 4:4-8 (ESV)*

Esther was stunned. She knew it was illegal to go to the king without being summoned, and she relayed this information to Mordecai. It's after Esther says, *"I can't do that,"* that Mordecai says his famous words.

> *Then Mordecai told them to reply to Esther, "Do not think to yourself that in the king's palace you will escape any more than all the other Jews. For if you keep silent at this time, relief and deliverance will rise for the Jews from another place, but you and your father's house will perish.*

And who knows whether you have not come to the kingdom for such a time as this?" -Esther 4:13-14 (ESV)

But he doesn't stop there—after Esther accepts his challenge to go to the king, Mordecai organizes all of the Jews to fast and pray for Esther. (Esther 4:16-27)

Later, when God answers their prayer and turns the king's heart, Mordecai is seen once again advising Esther and working alongside her to save their people. (Esther 9-10)

Now you may be asking, *"Great story. But what does all of this have to do with being a game-changing man of God?"*

Trust me, it has a connection. Too often, men who are broken and in need of healing from their own hurts have misused Scripture to silence, control, and oppress the women around them. Rather than learning the truth that a proper reading of the Bible shows that Judeo-Christian values have been the historic leaders in promoting dignity and value in women, these men have allowed broken egos and insecurities to keep women from walking into their God-given responsibilities, destinies, and callings.

This is not God's will, and it is not Biblical.

As we read in the Gospels, Jesus set the example of treating women with dignity and respect, encouraging them to hear His teaching, and allowing them to play a role in His ministry. He even gave a woman the honor of being the first one to see His resurrected body and share the good news of what she had seen.

Yet even before Jesus, we have Biblical examples of godly men encouraging women to be who God called them to be and do what God called them to do. Mordecai is one of these men.

As a follower of God, Mordecai recognized that God's plan to save His people would come through his niece. He knew that God had prepared Esther and arranged the details of her life for precisely this moment.

He didn't think, *"We need a man for this job."* Instead, he knew that his girl, his adopted daughter, was the one God chose.

So he challenged her.

He encouraged her and said, *"You can do this…you have to do this."*

He supported her by organizing the prayer and fasting. He was her cheerleader on the sidelines, saying, *"You can do this. God will help you, and you can save God's people."*

This is the heart and attitude that resides inside every game-changing man of God.

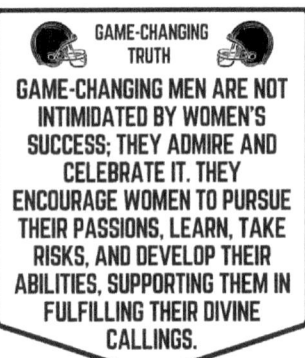

GAME-CHANGING TRUTH

GAME-CHANGING MEN ARE NOT INTIMIDATED BY WOMEN'S SUCCESS; THEY ADMIRE AND CELEBRATE IT. THEY ENCOURAGE WOMEN TO PURSUE THEIR PASSIONS, LEARN, TAKE RISKS, AND DEVELOP THEIR ABILITIES, SUPPORTING THEM IN FULFILLING THEIR DIVINE CALLINGS.

Here's the thing: Because a game-changing man has already dealt with any brokenness inside of them, they are not afraid of strong women. They don't see women as competition or a threat. Rather, they genuinely love their wives, their daughters, their mothers, and their sisters (including sisters in Christ), and they want to see them reach the full potential that God has for them.

They are not intimidated by women's success; they admire and celebrate it. They encourage women to pursue their passions, learn, take risks, and develop their abilities, supporting them in fulfilling their divine callings. They create an environment of growth, confidence, and encouragement. Recognizing that men and women are equally called to serve in God's kingdom, they support women in fulfilling their unique purposes, knowing this strengthens relationships, fosters growth, and advances God's plan. So they encourage and support the women around them to do all that God calls them to do.

When we read the book of Esther, we discover something powerful: the salvation of God's people began with one man who looked at a young woman and said with confidence, *"My girl can do it."*

Mordecai recognized the call of God on Esther's life. He didn't stand in her way. He didn't dismiss her because of her age, gender, or background. Instead, he believed in her, challenged her, and called her to rise up for such a time as this.

This raises an important question for us today: *Do you have this attitude toward the women in your life?*

Are you a game-changing man who wants to see your wife, daughter, sister, coworkers, and every woman God has placed in your life reach their full potential?

Do you long to see them walk in their gifts, fulfill their callings, and make a difference in the world? Or do you hold back, letting fear, pride, or cultural norms keep you from supporting them?

GAME-CHANGING TRUTH

BEING A GAME-CHANGING MAN MEANS SUPPORTING, ENCOURAGING, CHALLENGING, AND CHEERING FOR THE WOMEN IN YOUR LIFE.

Mordecai's example points us to an even greater example…Jesus. Jesus consistently elevated women, honored their faith, trusted them with kingdom assignments, and invited them to serve alongside Him. He spoke dignity into the woman at the well (John 4:1-42), defended the woman caught in adultery (John 8:1-11), entrusted the first announcement of His resurrection to Mary (Mark 16:9-12), and welcomed women as disciples in a culture that marginalized them

(Luke 8:1-3; 10:38-42). If the Son of God lifted women up, how can we as men do anything less?

Being a game-changing man means supporting, encouraging, challenging, and cheering for the women in your life. It means having the courage to say, *"God's hand is on you, and I will stand with you as you step into His calling."*

So let me ask you again: Do you have this kind of game-changing love and courage?

If your honest answer is *"no,"* then what practical steps will you take to grow into this kind of man? Maybe it means repenting of past attitudes or words that tore down instead of built up.

It may mean listening more deeply to the women in your life and affirming their God-given gifts.

Maybe it means intentionally mentoring your daughter in her calling, supporting your wife's dreams, or using your influence to open doors for women who have been overlooked.

Here's the truth: God never designed men and women to be enemies, competitors, or rivals. He never called us to dominate, silence, or devalue one another.

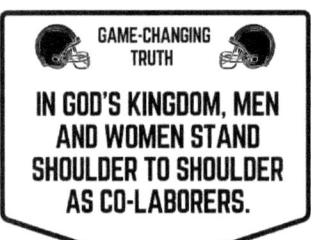

GAME-CHANGING TRUTH

IN GOD'S KINGDOM, MEN AND WOMEN STAND SHOULDER TO SHOULDER AS CO-LABORERS.

In God's kingdom, men and women stand shoulder to shoulder as co-laborers. Every single person is born with unique talents, abilities, and gifts handcrafted by God to accomplish His purposes. A game-changing man doesn't feel threatened by this. He celebrates it. He makes space for it. He champions it because he knows that when the women around him rise up in their callings, the kingdom of God moves forward with greater strength.

Just like Jesus and Mordecai, we can empower the women in our lives to be themselves, grow, and shine in the areas God guides them. As we work together and serve one another, we can put an end to the battle of the sexes and become a strong, game-changing team.

Together, we can change the world.

Dear Heavenly Father,

Thank You for the example of Mordecai, who believed in Esther's calling, and for Jesus, Who honored and empowered women to serve in Your kingdom. Forgive me for the times I've failed to support, encourage, or affirm the women in my life. Remove pride, fear, or passivity from my heart, and replace them with courage, humility, and love.

Help me to see my wife, daughters, sisters, coworkers, and friends as You see them—full of worth, gifts, and purpose. Teach me to speak life over them, celebrate their victories, and stand beside them as they walk in their callings. Give me courage to use my influence to open doors and create space for their voices.

Lord, shape me into a game-changing man who champions women, reflects the heart of Jesus, and strengthens Your kingdom by lifting women up. May my life encourage the women around me to reach their full potential in all that You created them to be.

In Jesus' name, Amen.

GROUP STUDY QUESTIONS:

1. What does Mordecai's encouragement to Esther, *"Perhaps you've come to the kingdom for such a time as this,"* teach us about the power of believing in a woman's calling?

2. Do you tend to encourage the women in your life to step into God's calling, or do you sometimes hold back?

3. What are some attitudes that may keep you from cheering them on?

4. How did Jesus' interactions with women break cultural norms? What lessons can you apply from His example in your own relationships?

5. What would your family, church, or workplace look like if men and women truly lived as equal partners in God's mission? How can you personally contribute to creating that culture?

6. Do you ever feel threatened, overlooked, or insecure when someone else—especially a woman—uses their gifts?

7. How can you surrender those feelings to God and replace them with celebration and partnership?

8. After reading this chapter, what is one thing you will put into practice or one thing you will change in your life?

9. How can we, as a group, help you do this?

CHAPTER FIVE
PROVE ME WRONG

It was a bright, clear Fall afternoon. The sky was so blue that I commented to my sister that it looked just like the sky on 9/11. We wrapped up work for the day, and I was on my back porch texting with a friend and fellow pastor about our fantasy football teams when the conversation shifted suddenly.

His next text was: *"Charlie Kirk just got shot at a college campus event. Not sure how he is. Just happened."*

What? A few moments later, I saw a video I wish I had never seen. A short time later, the President announced that Charlie Kirk had died.

So, here's the thing, until this day, I wasn't a follower of Charlie Kirk. I wasn't for or against him; I'm just a busy guy, and I don't fall into the demographic he reached. But after the shooting, I started watching videos of him debating students on college campuses. What stayed with me more than anything was his ability to answer questions and discuss theology and apologetics.

Time after time, a student would ask a question like, *"How do you know the Bible is accurate?"* or *"Why do you believe what the Bible says about the resurrection is true?"*. Each time, Charlie provided answers. Real answers. More than *"I feel it in my heart"* or *"Because the Bible says so."* Instead, he delivered logical, theological, and historical reasoning in a casual, conversational style.

As I watched, it reminded me of the story of the Apostle Paul in Athens in Acts 17.

> ***While Paul was waiting for them in Athens, he was greatly distressed to see that the city was full of idols. So he reasoned in the synagogue with both Jews and God-fearing Greeks, as well as in the marketplace day by day with those who happened to be there. -Acts 17:16-17 (NIV)***

Paul was in Athens waiting for Timothy and Silas. While he was there, he was brokenhearted as he looked around the city and saw so many people deceived and worshipping false gods rather than the One True God. So, he went to the local synagogue (Jewish place of worship) and started speaking to the Jews and God-fearing Gentiles. The word used here for *"reasoning"* actually means *"to reason, discuss, discourse; to argue, dispute."*[1] Every day, he *"reasoned"* or debated Christianity in the public square.

Here's some important background that will provide context for this story. At this time, Athens was home to two rival schools of philosophy: Epicureanism and Stoicism. These two philosophies represented the popular Greek alternatives for addressing the plight of humanity and for coming to terms with life outside of the Biblical truth of Jesus.[2]

Look at what happened next:

> *A group of Epicurean and Stoic philosophers began to debate with him. Some of them asked, "What is this babbler trying to say?" Others remarked, "He seems to be advocating foreign gods." They said this because Paul was preaching the good news about Jesus and the resurrection.*
>
> *Then they took him and brought him to a meeting of the Areopagus, where they said to him, "May we know what this new teaching is that you are presenting?*
>
> *You are bringing some strange ideas to our ears, and we would like to know what they mean."*
>
> *(All the Athenians and the foreigners who lived there spent their time doing nothing but talking about and listening to the latest ideas.) -Acts 17:18-21 (NIV)*

The Areopagus (meaning *"Council of Ares"*) was the senate or city council of a Greek city-state. In Roman times, it was the chief judicial body of the city, exercising jurisdiction in matters such as religion and education.

This is where the Epicureans and Stoics brought Paul—probably half in contemptuous mockery—but not really seeking truth. The city fathers, however, took their task seriously, as Athens was renowned for its debating of competing philosophies. To some degree, Paul's appearance before these men would determine whether or not he had permission to speak in their city.[2]

Here's where Paul's answer got interesting. Rather than using Jewish illustrations that the people of Athens wouldn't care about or understand, he begins his debate by referencing an altar with the inscription *"To an Unknown God."*

> *Paul then stood up in the meeting of the Areopagus and said: "People of Athens! I see that in every way you are very*

religious. For as I walked around and looked carefully at your objects of worship, I even found an altar with this inscription: to an unknown god. So you are ignorant of the very thing you worship—and this is what I am going to proclaim to you.

"The God who made the world and everything in it is the Lord of heaven and earth and does not live in temples built by human hands. And he is not served by human hands, as if he needed anything. Rather, he himself gives everyone life and breath and everything else.

From one man he made all the nations, that they should inhabit the whole earth; and he marked out their appointed times in history and the boundaries of their lands. God did this so that they would seek him and perhaps reach out for him and find him, though he is not far from any one of us. 'For in him we live and move and have our being.' As some of your own poets have said, 'We are his offspring.'

"Therefore since we are God's offspring, we should not think that the divine being is like gold or silver or stone— an image made by human design and skill. In the past God overlooked such ignorance, but now he commands all people everywhere to repent. For he has set a day when he will judge the world with justice by the man he has appointed. He has given proof of this to everyone by raising him from the dead." -Acts 17:22-31 (NIV)

Rather than quoting Old Testament prophets, Paul quotes two Greek poets: the Cretan poet Epimenides and the Cilician poet Aratus.

Using language and references his listeners would understand, Paul laid out a logical, relatable, yet theologically sound and Biblical argument for Christianity.

Look at the response:

> ***When they heard about the resurrection of the dead, some of them sneered, but others said, "We want to hear you again on this subject." At that, Paul left the Council. Some of the people became followers of Paul and believed. Among them was Dionysius, a member of the Areopagus, also a woman named Damaris, and a number of others.***
> ***-Acts 17:32-34 (NIV)***

This was the goal of Paul's teaching: to bring people to Jesus. In Athens, he achieved this goal by discussing topics that were familiar.

When speaking to a Jewish audience, he taught them about salvation and Jesus Christ, referencing Jewish history, the Old Testament Law, and demonstrating how Jesus fulfilled Messianic prophecies.

In Acts 14:14-18, we see that Paul spoke to the people of Lystra, who were probably peasants living in less developed areas, unfamiliar with Judaism or Greek philosophy, by talking about the God Who created the world and sends rain to help crops grow in season.

However, whenever and wherever Paul used words, he always ensured that people could relate to them as he explained the Gospel of Christ clearly.

If we are going to be game-changing men who influence the world around us for Jesus, we need to follow their example. This is why all men who want to share and defend their faith conversationally and change their world for Jesus must have a basic knowledge of theology and apologetics.

"Whoa, Jamie, that just took a sharp turn! I was not expecting that! Why is that important?"

Basically, you don't share what you don't understand. If you want to share your faith with others, then you need to have a basic understanding of what you're talking about.

"But isn't it enough just to share my testimony?"

Sometimes, but not always.

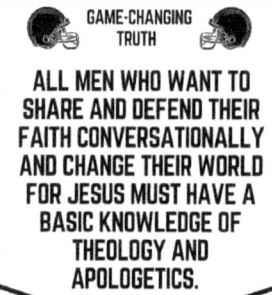

GAME-CHANGING TRUTH

ALL MEN WHO WANT TO SHARE AND DEFEND THEIR FAITH CONVERSATIONALLY AND CHANGE THEIR WORLD FOR JESUS MUST HAVE A BASIC KNOWLEDGE OF THEOLOGY AND APOLOGETICS.

The fact is that we live in a world where it isn't always enough to state a truth. Often, we must be able to defend it and explain it. In a technologically advanced age where most knowledge can be accessed with a few clicks, many people want further information. They want to ask questions and understand why or how something works. This doesn't mean they are hostile—it means they are seeking information and truth.

Knowing this fact, we must prepare ourselves to answer their questions.

As 1 Peter says:

> *But in your hearts revere Christ as Lord. Always be prepared to give an answer to everyone who asks you to give the reason for the hope that you have. But do this with gentleness and respect. -1 Peter 3:15 (NIV)*

"But Jamie, I'm not the Apostle Paul or Charlie Kirk. I'll never have that platform. Why do I need to know these things?"

Let me share three reasons:

1. **Godly men need to know theology and apologetics so they can pass the truth on to their children.**

> *Start children off on the way they should go, and even when they are old they will not turn from it. -Proverbs 22:6 (NIV)*

This is such a popular Scripture. However, it means more than just taking your kids to church. Instead, it places the responsibility on parents to teach their children Biblical truth.

Deuteronomy 6:4-9 lays the responsibility squarely on parents to teach their children God's ways.

> *Hear, O Israel: The Lord our God, the Lord is one.*
>
> *Love the Lord your God with all your heart and with all your soul and with all your strength.*
>
> *These commandments that I give you today are to be on your hearts. Impress them on your children.*
>
> *Talk about them when you sit at home and when you walk along the road, when you lie down and when you get up.*
>
> *Tie them as symbols on your hands and bind them on your foreheads.*
>
> *Write them on the doorframes of your houses and on your gates. (NIV)*

Notice that if you jump down to Deuteronomy 6:20-35, it says, *In the future, when your son asks you, "What is the meaning of the stipulations, decrees and laws the Lord our God has commanded you?" tell him: "We were slaves of Pharaoh in Egypt, but the Lord brought us out of Egypt with a mighty hand.*

Before our eyes the Lord sent signs and wonders—great and terrible—on Egypt and Pharaoh and his whole household. But he brought us out from there to bring us in and give us the land he promised on oath to our ancestors. The Lord commanded us to obey all these decrees and to fear the Lord our God, so that we might always prosper and be kept alive, as is the case today. And if we are careful to obey all this law before the Lord our God, as he has commanded us, that will be our righteousness." (NIV)

Right there, it says that when your child asks, "*Why do we follow God the way we do? What do His Laws mean? Why is this true?*" it is a godly parent's responsibility to answer the question.

This can only happen if you first understand why you believe what you believe and how you can explain it.

2. Godly men need to know theology and apologetics so they can answer the questions of unbelievers.

Somewhere along the line, the church got the mistaken idea that people will come to Jesus when some magical revival makes them want to go to church. There, they will hear a sermon or fall under the power of the Holy Spirit, and the altars will be filled with converts as the worship team plays.

But this isn't realistic. The fact is that most people come to Christ through conversations. Most people come to church because they are invited.

That's why it's essential that, even if we don't have a worldwide platform like Charlie Kirk or serve as a missionary or church leader like Paul, we understand theology and apologetics. All of us know people who don't have a personal relationship with Jesus. Since our lives carry influence, it's essential that we understand theology and apologetics so we can share truth with clarity and confidence.

In a world filled with secular humanism, philosophies, and false religions, many of these people want to know, *"Why do you believe that Christianity is the only way to Heaven? How do you know what you believe is the truth?"*

While some seek to argue or ridicule, others genuinely strive for the truth. Sometimes they aren't even the people asking the questions, but the ones listening as you talk to another person. Like the parable of the soils teaches us, it's not our job to judge soil; it's our job to plant seeds. (Matthew 13:1-23)

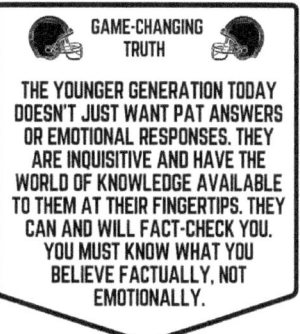

The younger generation today doesn't just want pat answers or emotional responses. They are inquisitive and have the world of knowledge available to them at their fingertips. They can and will fact-check you. You must know what you believe factually, not emotionally.

When someone approaches you with questions about our faith, it's your responsibility to have an answer for them. Knowing that we are men on a mission to reach people for Jesus, we must prepare ourselves for conversations by studying fundamental theology and being ready to explain and answer questions. We need to realize that it isn't about debate but about where a soul spends eternity.

3. Godly men need to know theology and apologetics so they can avoid false teachings and help their churches do the same.

From the beginning of the Church, false teachings have been a problem. Twisting and distorting God's Word is one of the enemy's most potent weapons against God's people. Browse through the New Testament and you'll see that almost every book addresses this topic in one way or another.

False teaching remains a significant problem in the Church today. It usually happens like this:

A popular new trend sweeps through the church world. Some celebrity pastor or influencer gets an idea, writes a book or holds a conference, and shares their unbiblical theories with all who will listen.

Even though these teachings aren't Biblical, they sound remarkably similar to the Bible. Using proof-texting (taking Scriptures out of context to support their point), they claim to be preaching truth even as they are spouting lies.

The problem is that because they are popular, funny, attractive, or promise health, wealth, and wisdom, people fall for it. Someone hears their message and passes the video, the meme, or the book onto a friend. Suddenly, everyone in the congregation is embracing false teaching because, well, everyone else is doing it.

One of the things that today's Church needs more than anything else is men who understand theology and apologetics enough to recognize when a false teaching begins to spread and say, *"Stop. This is not Biblical truth."* Then they need to be able to explain why.

Now more than ever, I genuinely believe that we need game-changing men who will pick up the call to follow the instructions that Paul gave to Timothy:

> *The Spirit clearly says that in later times some will abandon the faith and follow deceiving spirits and things taught by demons. Such teachings come through hypocritical liars, whose consciences have been seared as with a hot iron. They forbid people to marry and order them to abstain from certain foods, which God created to be received with thanksgiving by those who believe and who know the truth. For everything God created is good, and*

nothing is to be rejected if it is received with thanksgiving, because it is consecrated by the word of God and prayer.

If you point these things out to the brothers and sisters, you will be a good minister of Christ Jesus, nourished on the truths of the faith and of the good teaching that you have followed. -1 Timothy 4:1-6 (NIV)

Do you want to be a trustworthy man who avoids false teachings and helps others do the same? It begins with building a foundational knowledge of theology and apologetics.

At this point, you may be asking,

"Alright, I hear what you're saying. But how do I get started?"

The first thing you want to do is avoid being overwhelmed. Don't think *"This is too much to learn. I don't know where I'd even start. Besides, it's over my head. It's just too hard".*

These are lies from the enemy who doesn't want to see you unleash your full potential. With the help of the Holy Spirit, you can read, learn, and understand theology.

Rather than feeling overwhelmed, remember, *"How do you eat an elephant? One bite at a time."* [3]

The journey to learning theology and apologetics starts one step at a time. Here are some ideas to get started.

1. Read the Assemblies of God *16 Fundamental Truths*. Don't just read the short version. Read the extended version and look up the Scriptures. This will help you gain a solid understanding of the essential things every Christian needs to know.

2. Read through Mantour Ministries' book *"Legendary Truths"*. It contains 52 devotionals that break down fundamental truths into bite-sized nuggets of truth. It's a great introduction to theology. Although it was originally written for men, the content can be used by anyone or worked through as a family.

3. **Read *"Bible Doctrines: A Pentecostal Perspective"* by William W. Menzies and Stanley M. Horton.** This book expands on the *16 Fundamental Truths* and is easy to read.

4. **Read *"Systematic Theology: A Pentecostal Perspective"* by Stanley Horton.** This book is a little deeper and more in-depth than *"Bible Doctrines: A Pentecostal Perspective"*; however, it isn't overly academic.

5. **Check out the YouTube playlist *Theology Matters* by Assemblies of God USA.**

6. **The Assemblies of God website (www.ag.org)** has videos and articles that dive deeper into the *16 Fundamental Truths* and additional teachings about the Cardinal Doctrines of Salvation, Baptism in the Holy Spirit, Divine Healing, and the Second Coming of Christ. These free resources will help you learn more about each topic.

7. **Many churches have a School of Ministry that offers theology classes.** This is a great opportunity to learn more. Ask your pastor what's available.

8. **One by one, read through the *Assemblies of God Position Papers*.** Addressing many questions, they provide a Scripture basis for why we believe what we believe.

9. **Take an online course.** Global University offers theology classes online. Turning Point USA offers a free online course called *"First Truths,"* a six-part cornerstone course that teaches the foundational doctrines of the Christian faith.

For Apologetics:

1. TPUSA offers a free class with Dr. Frank Turk called "Defending the Faith". I took the class and found it very informative and helpful.

2. Read Dr. Frank Turek's book, *"I Don't Have Enough Faith to Be An Atheist."*

3. Read John Cooper's book, *"Awake & Alive to Truth: Finding Truth in the Chaos of a Relativistic World"*

4. Read Alicia Childers' books:

- *Another Gospel?: A Lifelong Christian Seeks Truth in Response to Progressive Christianity*

- *Live Your Truth and Other Lies: Exposing Popular Deceptions That Make Us Anxious, Exhausted, and Self-Obsessed*

- *The Deconstruction of Christianity: What It Is, Why It's Destructive, and How to Respond*

5. Read *"A Grand Illusion: How Progressive Christianity Undermines Biblical Faith"* **by David Young.**

6. Read *"Fault Lines: The Social Justice Movement and Evangelicalism's Looming Catastrophe"* **by Voddie Baucham Jr.**

7. CrossExamined.org is a non-profit ministry founded in 2006 that conducts dynamic seminars on college campuses, in churches, and in high schools. Led by Frank Turek and other Christian apologists. It exists to address the questions of the intellectually skeptical. They offer books, articles, online courses, and even curricula to teach your children.

Most importantly, I encourage you to take the first step forward. Don't think that theology and apologetics are just for pastors or those with major platforms. No, our world needs game-changing men who know what they believe and can share it conversationally with others to make a difference in their lives.

That man could be you!

Dear Heavenly Father,

I come before You humbled, realizing how much I need to grow in my understanding of Your Word. I don't want to simply have shallow answers when people ask me about my faith; I want to be ready with truth, wisdom, and clarity that points them back to You. Give me the hunger to study and the discipline to learn so I can be prepared to defend what I believe. More than just head knowledge, I ask that everything I learn would sink deep into my heart so it shapes the way I live and the way I love others.

Father, help me to follow Paul's example of reasoning with people and sharing truth in a way they can understand. Give me boldness to speak, gentleness to listen, and wisdom to discern what to say in each moment. Protect me from pride or arrogance, and let every conversation I have be filled with respect, compassion, and the power of Your Spirit. Above all, I pray that my words would draw people closer to You and that my life would reflect the hope I have in Christ. In Jesus' Name, Amen

GROUP STUDY QUESTIONS:

1. Why do you think Paul chose to use cultural references (like Greek poets and the *"Unknown God"* altar) instead of Jewish Scripture when speaking in Athens? What does this teach us about sharing our faith today?

2. In what ways do theology (knowing what we believe) and apologetics (defending why we believe it) work together to strengthen our witness?

3. The passage compared Charlie Kirk's debating style to Paul's approach in Acts 17. What lessons can we take from their conversational methods of answering questions about faith?

4. According to 1 Peter 3:15, Christians are called to give an answer for the hope they have *"with gentleness and respect."* What are some practical ways we can live this out in everyday conversations?

5. Why is it important for godly men to pass down theological truth to their children, and how can we make this a daily practice at home?

6. How can knowing theology and apologetics help us recognize and resist false teachings that may look *"Biblical"* but are not grounded in truth?

7. What first step can you personally take this week to grow in your knowledge of theology and apologetics so that you can better share and defend your faith?

8. How can we, as a group, help you do this?

CHAPTER SIX
THE MAN BEHIND THE MAN

In the Netflix series' *Quarterbacks* and *Receivers*, we see the superstars of the gridiron shine under the bright lights. We watch the throws, the catches, the highlights, the touchdowns. But behind every highlight is a hidden reality—an army of trainers, physical therapists, and recovery staff working relentlessly behind the scenes. These men and women stretch muscles, ice joints, patch injuries, and build custom rehab plans to keep these athletes on the field.

They aren't on camera often. They don't get interviewed. No one knows their names outside of the locker room. But they are absolutely pivotal. Without them, the quarterback doesn't make it to Sunday. Without them, the wide receiver never makes it past Monday.

These trainers reflect a spiritual truth every game-changing man must understand: health and strength don't happen by accident—they are sustained by intentional support.

As men, we often want to be the ones out front, making the play, leading the charge, taking the hit. However, even the best warriors need a team around them—people who support them in maintaining their spiritual, emotional, and physical well-being. The Christian walk isn't meant to be walked alone.

Very few men get called to be the man out front, the one everyone notices. However, every man in this role will tell you they are not the key figures. They couldn't do what they do without a support team around them, helping them, guiding them, being their strength, and making their load more manageable. No man can do it alone.

Often, we think that if we are not the one in front, we don't matter. However, the man we are going to look at today shows us the exact opposite. A game-changing man is a man who supports and encourages leaders, who has their back in good times and bad. Let's take a look at what I mean as we look at the life of a man named Silas. Silas' journey starts before we even read his name in the Bible. Let's look at some background information that led him to the scene.

> *Now there were in the church at Antioch prophets and teachers, Barnabas, Simeon who was called Niger, Lucius of Cyrene, Manaen a lifelong friend of Herod the tetrarch, and Saul.*
>
> *While they were worshiping the Lord and fasting, the Holy Spirit said, "Set apart for me Barnabas and Saul for the work to which I have called them." Then after fasting and praying they laid their hands on them and sent them off.*
>
> *So, being sent out by the Holy Spirit, they went down to Seleucia, and from there they sailed to Cyprus. When they arrived at Salamis, they proclaimed the word of God in the*

> *synagogues of the Jews. And they had John (Mark) to assist them. -Acts 13:1-5 (ESV)*

God handpicked Paul and Barnabas to go far and wide and preach the Gospel. John Mark, or Mark as he is usually known, was sent along as their assistant. He would serve alongside them and attend to all their needs. However, things didn't go quite as planned.

> *Now Paul and his companions set sail from Paphos and came to Perga in Pamphylia. And John left them and returned to Jerusalem, -Acts 13:13 (ESV)*

Although the passage appears to state that Mark simply went home, a deeper implication exists. He didn't return because he was no longer needed…he abandoned them. He ran away and left them alone without a younger man to help them.

It is important to realize his job description.

Paul and Barnabas were probably middle-aged men. Everywhere they went, they went on foot. They had to carry their own supplies. They had to protect themselves from animals and thieves. This was probably the reason why a strapping young guy like Mark was sent along. He was to be their muscle, their pack horse, their physical support as they did their spiritual work.

When he abandoned them, they were forced to pick up his responsibilities and balance both the spiritual and physical work, bearing the weight and exhaustion that accompanied each set of duties. Fortunately, they met another young man named Timothy, who picked up Mark's responsibilities.

The trip ultimately proved to be a huge success, as people accepted Christ and churches were planted at each stop. Paul and Barnabas returned from their successful missionary trip and began planning another journey to check on the new converts. As the two men began making plans, an argument erupted between them.

> *And after some days Paul said to Barnabas, "Let us return and visit the brothers in every city where we proclaimed the word of the Lord, and see how they are." Now Barnabas wanted to take with them John called Mark. But Paul thought best not to take with them one who had withdrawn from them in Pamphylia and had not gone with them to the work. And there arose a sharp disagreement, so that they separated from each other. -Acts 15:36-39 (ESV)*

Paul was not about to take Mark back out on the road again. Mark had already quit on him once! He was not going through that again.

On the other hand, Barnabas had a desire to help Mark and restore him to a place of usefulness in God's service. He saw Mark's potential, and he wanted to help him reach it. As a result, Paul and Barnabas went their separate ways.

> *Barnabas took Mark with him and sailed away to Cyprus, but Paul chose Silas and departed, having been commended by the brothers to the grace of the Lord. -Acts 15:39-40 (ESV)*

Paul chose Silas to go with him to minister to the Gentiles. Barnabas chose Mark to accompany him, and they ministered to the Jews.

Ultimately, it was a good thing because twice the ground was covered and twice the people were reached. But at the moment, this was a huge deal! Paul wanted to take the trip, and he needed someone to accompany him, to be his assistant, if you will, to help him do what God had called him to do. That's where we meet Silas.

Silas was a leader of the Jerusalem congregation, and he had been sent by the Jewish leaders, along with Paul and Barnabas, to deliver a letter explaining the apostles' view on what was required for Gentiles to become converts. Hint: it wasn't circumcision, as false teachers were teaching. Silas was a trusted leader known to both the Jewish and Gentile churches. He also, like Paul, had dual citizenship with Israel and Rome, so he could also claim his Roman citizenship when attacked or imprisoned.

Ultimately, God provided Silas to help Paul. He wasn't chosen for his fame or charisma—he was selected because he had proven himself trustworthy, dependable, and Spirit-filled. That's the kind of man Paul needed, not a celebrity, not a crowd-pleaser, but a steady, loyal brother who would walk with him through thick and thin.

Silas became that man. He didn't just travel with Paul—he endured with Paul. He was there when Paul was beaten and imprisoned in Philippi. He was there in the midnight hour, singing hymns in chains.(Acts 16:16-40) He was there when the gospel was rejected in Thessalonica. (Acts 17:1-9) Silas didn't demand recognition. He didn't insist on leading the charge. Instead, he threw his weight behind the mission, supported Paul as God's appointed leader, and advanced the gospel through his faithfulness. Silas showed us that game-changing men don't have to be in the spotlight to change the game—they change it by lifting up the leaders God has placed before them.

Game-changing men today can learn a lot from Silas. Every leader—whether a pastor, coach, teacher, boss, or father—needs men willing to come alongside them.

This is what game-changing men do today. They understand that leadership is often a lonely, exhausting, and underappreciated role. They recognize that leaders are often open to attack. They don't sit on the sidelines critiquing the man out front. They step in beside him, offering encouragement, carrying part of the burden, and reminding him he's not fighting alone. A true game changer doesn't just ask, *"What can I get from my leader?"* Instead, he asks, *"What can I give to strengthen him, so that together we accomplish what God has called us to?"*

Think about the impact of Silas. Without him, Paul's ministry could have stalled after his split with Barnabas. However, because Silas came alongside, the gospel advanced, churches were planted, and the kingdom grew. Silas literally helped change world history.

I know God has blessed me with men like Silas over the years. I recall a few years after we started Mantours, a man approached me at a conference. He was in his early sixties, and he told me that God told him to help us at each Mantour. At this point, I wasn't receiving a salary for Mantour Conferences, so I couldn't pay him. So for years, he would come to the Mantours on his own dime, sometimes traveling to other states, and help. He would carry boxes, set up displays, work behind the table, whatever he needed, he did. He did this as long as he could until his age caught up with him. He was a blessing to a young ministry and to me.

Fast forward a few years. My physical health was deteriorating, and I needed help desperately. I could barely walk anymore, and the pain of doing the Mantours was excruciating, usually taking days to recover, only to hit the road again and start the pain cycle all over again. I thought I had found someone to help us and lessen the burden, but this guy quit and left me high and dry. I kinda get how Paul felt when Mark left.

But like Paul, God raised up a Silas to help. A good friend and fellow minister stepped up. He became a Silas to me, traveling to Mantours and doing the physical work that I cannot do, allowing me to focus on the ministry while not suffering physically. He has been a

Godsend, having a willingness to serve behind the scenes in any way possible.

The world and the church need more men like this man and like Silas.

Guys, not everyone is called to be a Paul, but every man can be a Silas. Every man can choose to stand in the trenches with his pastor, his mentor, his leader, and say, *"You're not walking this road alone."*

Even as I lead Mantour Ministries and do what God called me to do, I am also a Silas to another leader. I help him in ways that I won't mention, because I don't honestly want to be recognized for it. However, I support him in his ministry and help him reach more people as I work behind the scenes, doing things he isn't equipped to do but need to be done in today's culture. I don't say this for praise or recognition. I say it to show that everyone, even leaders, can be a Silas to another man.

Silas prayed for Paul.

Silas showed us key ways to make a difference. One key way is through prayer. Silas didn't just stand silently next to Paul in chains. He lifted his voice in prayer and worship with him. In the darkest of hours, when others might have crumbled in fear or despair, Silas joined Paul in seeking God's presence. This partnership in prayer not only strengthened Paul, it shook the prison walls and opened the door for God's power to be displayed. (Acts 16:25-40)

Don't underestimate the impact of interceding for those God has placed over you. Pray for their strength when the weight of responsibility grows heavy. Pray for their family, that their home would be filled with peace and joy. Pray for their protection from spiritual attacks and discouragement. Pray for clarity of vision, that they would hear God's direction clearly and boldly walk in it. Your leader may carry the visible role, but your prayers help carry the unseen battles. Just as Silas lifted Paul in prayer and worship, game-changing men lift their leaders before God, standing in the gap with faith and persistence.

Silas encouraged Paul.

Leaders needed encouragement. It can be a lonely job as few celebrate victories, but many point out what they consider failures. A game-changing man is an encourager. Leaders have challenging, unseen problems. A kind word, a quick text, or just saying, *"I'm with you,"* can give them the strength to go on. Your small words of encouragement can help them lead better in front of others.

Silas was a supporter of Paul.

Every leader has people who criticize them. Game-changing men don't join in criticizing; they protect their leader's good name. They show love and avoid gossip or bad talk. They support them in both good and bad times. Look at Silas. Silas didn't abandon Paul when Paul was attacked or imprisoned. He was right there with him. He stayed with him when others turned away.

Silas helped carry the load.

Ministry and leadership can be demanding, often more than most people realize. Leaders carry not only their own responsibilities but also the weight of guiding others, making decisions, and standing firm when pressures mount. That's why the presence of supportive, game-changing men is so vital.

When you notice a gap, don't stand back…fill the gap. If your pastor seems worn out, don't wait for him or her to ask for help. Step up and volunteer your time, energy, or resources. If your boss is overwhelmed with deadlines and details, offer to shoulder part of the load.

THE MAN BEHIND THE MAN

Game-changing men don't sit on the sidelines waiting to be asked.

They develop an awareness of what's happening around them and recognize needs before anyone points them out. They understand that their role isn't just to lead when they're in charge but also to strengthen and uphold those who are leading. Real influence is found in seeing the need, stepping into the gap, and helping others carry the burden. What sets game-changing men apart is that they are dependable, take the initiative, and are eager to serve.

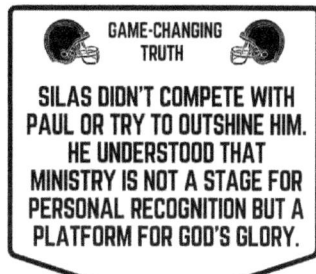

GAME-CHANGING TRUTH

SILAS DIDN'T COMPETE WITH PAUL OR TRY TO OUTSHINE HIM. HE UNDERSTOOD THAT MINISTRY IS NOT A STAGE FOR PERSONAL RECOGNITION BUT A PLATFORM FOR GOD'S GLORY.

Silas didn't compete with Paul or try to outshine him. He understood that ministry is not a stage for personal recognition but a platform for God's glory. Silas wasn't worried about his own name being remembered in history...what mattered to him was that the name of Jesus was lifted high. His joy came from watching the gospel advance, no matter who got the spotlight.

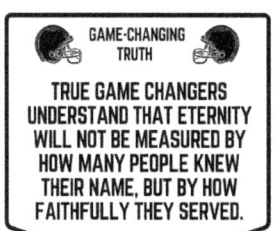

GAME-CHANGING TRUTH

TRUE GAME CHANGERS UNDERSTAND THAT ETERNITY WILL NOT BE MEASURED BY HOW MANY PEOPLE KNEW THEIR NAME, BUT BY HOW FAITHFULLY THEY SERVED.

That's the heart of a true game changer. They know it's not about credit, applause, or recognition. They are not pursuing influence for personal gain. Instead, they are using their influence to serve the kingdom. When others succeed, they celebrate. When someone else's name is remembered, they rejoice, because the mission is bigger than personal fame. True game changers understand that eternity will not be measured by how many people knew their name, but by how faithfully they served.

Think about the impact of Silas. Without him, Paul's ministry could have stalled after his split with Barnabas. But because Silas came alongside, the gospel advanced, churches were planted, and the kingdom grew. Supporting leadership doesn't just bless the leader—it multiplies the mission.

Game-changing men today need to be like Silas. Not everyone is called to be a Paul, but every man can be a Silas. Every man can choose to stand in the trenches with his pastor, his mentor, his leader, and say, *"You're not walking this road alone."*

For every Paul, there are a million Silases. The truth of the matter is that there really can't be a Paul without a Silas. Game-changing men realize this, and they step up and do all they can to support the leaders around them. Why? So that God's kingdom can grow.

Dear Heavenly Father,

Help me to have the heart of Silas. Keep me from competing with others or seeking to outshine them. Guard me from the temptation of chasing recognition, and remind me daily that ministry is not about building my name but lifting up Yours. Help me to be dependable, steady, and humble, always pointing people back to You. Let my life prove that true greatness is found in serving, and may everything I do advance Your Kingdom, not my own name. Amen.

Father, shape me into a true game changer—one who values Kingdom impact over personal applause. Let my influence be used not for my own gain but to strengthen others and glorify You. At the end of my life, I don't want to be remembered for how many people knew me, but for how faithfully I served You. May everything I do point to the name above every name, Jesus Christ, my Lord. In Jesus' name, Amen.

THE MAN BEHIND THE MAN

GROUP STUDY QUESTIONS:

1. Why do you think Silas was content to serve alongside Paul instead of competing with him?

2. What are some practical ways we can be like Silas and support the leaders God has placed in our lives?

3. How does celebrating others' success protect us from jealousy or pride?

4. What burdens do leaders in ministry or the workplace carry that we often overlook?

5. Think of a time when someone stepped in to support you. How did it make a difference in your life?

6. What steps can we take this week to actively encourage, strengthen, or help someone else in their calling?

7. After reading this chapter, what is one thing you will put into practice or one thing you will change in your life?

8. How can we, as a group, help you do this?

CHAPTER SEVEN
ATAH HA'ISH'ING AUTHORITY

Twenty-seven years ago, I did one of the hardest things I have ever done in my life. I took a class studying the Hebrew language. Every Pastoral Ministries major at my college was required to take either a Greek class or a Hebrew class. I chose Hebrew because I really liked the professor who taught the class. I should have taken Greek! It was HARD! I did not do well.

The language itself was difficult, but my beloved professor was doing doctoral work on the Hebrew language, and when he gave his first midterm to us, the ENTIRE CLASS failed!

Many students complained that the test was too hard. They spoke truth to authority even when it could have been risky. Thankfully, the professor listened to them. He ended up showing the test to his colleagues, who told him that the test was really unfair — it was geared toward graduate work, not first-year Hebrew students. Thankfully, he listened to those colleagues and rewrote the midterm.

I admit, twenty-seven years later, I remember very, very little from this class. To be honest, I only remember three Hebrew words…*Atah ha'ish* (האיש אתה), which translates to *"You are the Man."*

Of all the words to remember, this is it? Well, back in the day, *"You da man"* was a trendy thing to say, so this Hebrew phrase stuck in my head. Weird, I know.

I think about this every time I read about the man we are going to look at in this chapter. These words of *atah ha'ish* were spoken by him in 2 Samuel, and he used them like a bomb to blow up the web of lies, deceit, and murder by one of God's most trusted men. The man who spoke these words is truly game-changing because he was willing to speak the truth and stand for God and His ways, no matter the cost. So let's look at the life of Nathan.

Nathan was a prophet of God during the reign of David and his son, Solomon. We first read about Nathan in 2 Samuel 7. In this passage, King David decides he wants to build a holy temple for God, so that God will have a place to reside in Israel. David was excited. However, God wasn't 100% on board.

> *Now then, tell my servant David, 'This is what the Lord Almighty says: I took you from the pasture, from tending the flock, and appointed you ruler over my people Israel. I have been with you wherever you have gone, and I have cut off all your enemies from before you.*
>
> *Now I will make your name great, like the names of the greatest men on earth. And I will provide a place for my people Israel and will plant them so that they can have a home of their own and no longer be disturbed. Wicked people will not oppress them anymore, as they did at the beginning and have done ever*

since the time I appointed leaders over my people Israel. I will also give you rest from all your enemies.

"'The Lord declares to you that the Lord himself will establish a house for you: When your days are over and you rest with your ancestors, I will raise up your offspring to succeed you, your own flesh and blood, and I will establish his kingdom. He is the one who will build a house for my Name, and I will establish the throne of his kingdom forever. I will be his father, and he will be my son. When he does wrong, I will punish him with a rod wielded by men, with floggings inflicted by human hands. But my love will never be taken away from him, as I took it away from Saul, whom I removed from before you. Your house and your kingdom will endure forever before me; your throne will be established forever.'" -2 Samuel 7:8-16 (NIV)

Nathan was given the unenviable task of going and telling the king, the man with all the power, that he couldn't build the temple that his heart so desired. However, in this message from God, we hear what is known as the *David Covenant*, a promise from God that David and his family would always have a kingdom that would endure forever. This is, of course, fulfilled in the life of Jesus, the King of kings.

So Nathan told David the message. He boldly spoke the unpopular truth.

"Jamie, of course, it was okay that he told David this because he gave him this huge prophetic blessing. Would he still be willing to speak this way to the king if it would truly have been costly to him?"

Of course he would. As a game-changing man, Nathan knew obedience to God was more important than fear of man. Silence was never an option for him. We see this in his *atah ha'ish* moment.

Fast forward a few years. David has become complacent in his job as king. Instead of doing what he was supposed to do, leading the army in battle, David decided to stay at home alone and relax.

> *In the spring of the year, the time when kings go out to battle, David sent Joab, and his servants with him, and all Israel. And they ravaged the Ammonites and besieged Rabbah. But David remained at Jerusalem.*
>
> *It happened, late one afternoon, when David arose from his couch and was walking on the roof of the king's house, that he saw from the roof a woman bathing; and the woman was very beautiful.*
>
> *And David sent and inquired about the woman.*
>
> *And one said, "Is not this Bathsheba, the daughter of Eliam, the wife of Uriah the Hittite?"*
>
> *So David sent messengers and took her, and she came to him, and he lay with her. (Now she had been purifying herself from her uncleanness.) Then she returned to her house. And the woman conceived, and she sent and told David, "I am pregnant." -2 Samuel 11:1-5 (ESV)*

David gave way to his lust and had an affair with Bathsheba. Allow me to make a brief side point. We are quick to judge Bathsheba in the story, but all she did was take a bath. People say, *"Well, Jamie, she was bathing naked on her roof."* Are you sure that's in the Bible? Look again at 2 Samuel 11.

> *It happened, late one afternoon, when David arose from his couch and was walking on the roof of the king's*

> *house, that he saw from the roof a woman bathing; and the woman was very beautiful. -1 Samuel 11:2 (ESV)*

Notice, nowhere does it say she was a wily temptress doing a hoochie-coochie dance on her roof. It says David was looking at her FROM HIS ROOF. In reality, all it says is that Bathsheba was taking a bath. Moreover, it was a ceremonial bath, an act of worship, intended to purify herself. (1 Samuel 11:4) David sinned by lusting after her and degrading her. Nowhere does it say she seduced him. David was the Peeping Tom. It doesn't even say she was a willing party. After all, David was king. Did she even have an option in the matter?

Okay, back to the point of this chapter. David sins against God by being complacent in his calling, lusting, and committing adultery. He then forces a married woman to sleep with him, and then finds out she is pregnant. Oops! His secret sin was about to be exposed. In a desperate attempt to save face, David devises a plan.

He contacts his chief commander, Joab, and tells him to send Uriah, Bathsheba's husband, to him. How did David know who Uriah was? Well, in 1 Chronicles 11, we read a list of mighty warriors called *David's Mighty Men*. These men were the men who helped make David the King of Israel. Many of them were the men who came to David when he was on the run from Saul. They stood with him during his most difficult time. They fought beside him from the beginning and were mighty warriors. When you read this list, you find an interesting name.

> *Now these are the chiefs of David's mighty men, who gave him strong support in his kingdom, together with all Israel, to make him king, according to the word of the Lord concerning Israel...Uriah the Hittite. -1 Chronicles 11:10, 41 (ESV)*

Uriah was one of David's mighty men! He was one of David's most trusted warriors, a fierce and skilled fighter. He was out on the battlefield, fighting for David, while David was at home sleeping with his wife!

Joab sends Uriah to David, and Uriah tells David all about the battle. David, a total hypocrite, thanks his old battle friend and tells him to go home and spend some time with his wife, hoping Uriah will sleep with her, and then no one would know about the pregnancy.

But Uriah refused to do this. He was a loyal soldier, and he wouldn't enjoy his wife while his buddies were fighting. So David commits the ultimate form of betrayal against Uriah and his God.

> ***In the morning David wrote a letter to Joab and sent it by the hand of Uriah. In the letter he wrote, "Set Uriah in the forefront of the hardest fighting, and then draw back from him, that he may be struck down, and die." -2 Samuel 11:14-15 (ESV)***

David ordered the murder of a close friend and comrade, all to save his butt and keep his sin a secret. He took Bathsheba, made her marry him, and thought it was behind him. But God knew, and He told our man Nathan.

Can you imagine being Nathan in this situation? He had a job to do for God, and he had to do it. Or did he?

He could have chosen to remain silent. He could have looked the other way. It was very dangerous to confront David in the state of mind David was in. He had already basically killed a close friend. What was to stop him from killing his pastor for trying to expose him?

But Nathan was a game-changing man. He knew his fear couldn't lead him. He had to boldly speak for what is right, no matter the cost.

Nathan went to confront David.

> *And the Lord sent Nathan to David. He came to him and said to him, "There were two men in a certain city, the one rich and the other poor. The rich man had very many flocks and herds, but the poor man had nothing but one little ewe lamb, which he had bought. And he brought it up, and it grew up with him and with his children. It used to eat of his morsel and drink from his cup and lie in his arms, and it was like a daughter to him.*
>
> *Now there came a traveler to the rich man, and he was unwilling to take one of his own flock or herd to prepare for the guest who had come to him, but he took the poor man's lamb and prepared it for the man who had come to him."*
>
> *Then David's anger was greatly kindled against the man, and he said to Nathan, "As the Lord lives, the man who has done this deserves to die, and he shall restore the lamb fourfold, because he did this thing, and because he had no pity." -2 Samuel 12:1-6 (ESV)*

Nathan set David up with this story. He appealed to David's role as judge and decision-maker, presenting the case to him. David, not getting it, became angry. Nathan then goes for the kill shot.

> *Nathan said to David, "You are the man!*
>
> *Thus says the Lord, the God of Israel, 'I anointed you king over Israel, and I delivered you out of the hand of Saul. And I gave you your master's house and your master's wives into your arms and gave you the house of*

Israel and of Judah. And if this were too little, I would add to you as much more.

Why have you despised the word of the Lord, to do what is evil in his sight? You have struck down Uriah the Hittite with the sword and have taken his wife to be your wife and have killed him with the sword of the Ammonites. Now therefore the sword shall never depart from your house, because you have despised me and have taken the wife of Uriah the Hittite to be your wife.'

Thus says the Lord, 'Behold, I will raise up evil against you out of your own house. And I will take your wives before your eyes and give them to your neighbor, and he shall lie with your wives in the sight of this sun. For you did it secretly, but I will do this thing before all Israel and before the sun.'" -1 Samuel 12:7-12 (ESV)

Atah Ha'ish. You are the man! You are the one who stole Uriah's precious wife, then killed him to cover up your sin. You did it, King David!

Nathan spoke the unpopular truth to authority, knowing it could cost him everything. He exposed David's lies, causing David to crack, repent, and turn back to God. But Nathan didn't know this would be the result. For all he knew, David could have arranged for an accident to befall him like he did with Uriah. Yet he refused to stay silent! These are the actions of a game-changing man.

God is searching for men who will stand firm for Him, speaking truth to culture's lies and risking it all to stand by their convictions in a world that tries to silence and intimidate us.

Game-changing men resist the call to conformity and stand for God and His truth, no matter the cost. Nathan came through it with his head still attached to his body, but he had no way of knowing that would be the result. And sometimes it isn't.

We mentioned earlier in the book about the founder of Turning Point USA, and a fellow believer, Charlie Kirk, being assassinated, shot through the neck for standing by what he believed in. He was hated for his Christian convictions and for refusing to back down, and since they couldn't defeat him, they silenced him. Standing up for the truth involves risk, but a game-changing man accepts that risk.

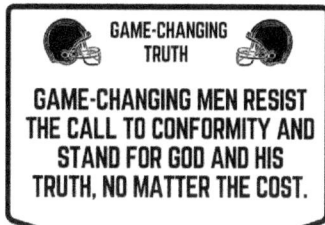

GAME-CHANGING TRUTH

GAME-CHANGING MEN RESIST THE CALL TO CONFORMITY AND STAND FOR GOD AND HIS TRUTH, NO MATTER THE COST.

"But Jamie, I will never be called upon to speak to the President, or to debate like Charlie. I'm just a regular guy living an everyday life."

You may be right. You may not be called to confront a king, but every man will face moments when truth must be spoken. These crossroads may not come with crowns and thrones, but they carry eternal weight.

- A friend drifting into destructive choices—getting tangled in addiction, walking into an affair, abandoning his family, or chasing quick thrills that will cost him everything. You know your silence could be the very thing that allows him to spiral deeper.

- A workplace where compromise is the norm—inflating numbers on reports, laughing off crude jokes to *"fit in,"* or being told to put profit above integrity. In those moments, the Spirit whispers, *"Stand apart. Don't sell out."*

- A culture that mocks God's standards—where pornography is normal, marriage is disposable, gender is confused, and purity is ridiculed. The world tells you to keep your faith to yourself, but you know silence only fuels the darkness.

- A family gathering where tension runs high—and it would be easier to bite your tongue than speak truth in love to a sibling, a child, or a parent who is straying from God's path.

- A church that avoids hard conversations, where everyone is comfortable but no one is being challenged, and you feel God calling you to say what others are afraid to voice.

- A society that celebrates what God calls sin…applauding greed, pride, selfishness, evil, and rebellion, while silencing anyone who dares to point back to God's Word.

In those moments, the easy road is silence. But silence is deadly. Silence allows sin to spread unchecked. Silence sacrifices conviction for comfort, and makes cowards where God is calling for game-changers.

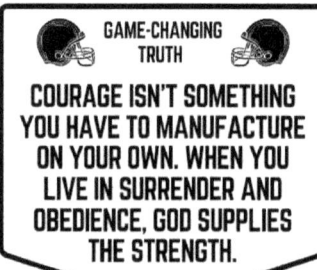

GAME-CHANGING TRUTH

COURAGE ISN'T SOMETHING YOU HAVE TO MANUFACTURE ON YOUR OWN. WHEN YOU LIVE IN SURRENDER AND OBEDIENCE, GOD SUPPLIES THE STRENGTH.

Game-changing men refuse to let fear dictate their lives. They understand that obeying God is worth the sacrifice, even if it means giving up approval, missing out on opportunities, or seeing relationships fall apart. Nathan stood before David, the most powerful man in the land, aware that one wrong word could be his last. But he also knew that disobeying God would be an even greater loss.

Here is the hope we have. The same Spirit Who filled Nathan and gave him boldness to speak truth to power lives in us today. Courage isn't something you have to manufacture on your own. When you live in surrender and obedience, God supplies the strength.

Guys, this world doesn't need more men who play it safe. It doesn't need more silence, excuses, or passive bystanders. It needs men who will stand in the gap, men who will speak God's truth when it is unpopular, and men who will call others back to holiness with conviction and compassion. It needs men who will rise up and declare: *"I will not be silent, no matter the cost."*

When fear tells us to stay quiet, a game-changing man remembers God's command to be strong and courageous, because God is with them (Joshua 1:9). When the enemy tempts us to hide, we must not forget that silence is deadly, but truth spoken in love brings life.

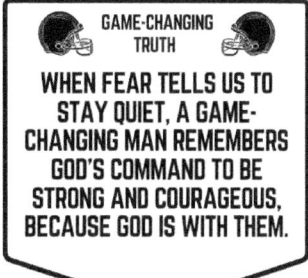

GAME-CHANGING TRUTH
WHEN FEAR TELLS US TO STAY QUIET, A GAME-CHANGING MAN REMEMBERS GOD'S COMMAND TO BE STRONG AND COURAGEOUS, BECAUSE GOD IS WITH THEM.

Nathan's courage led to David's repentance. David's repentance led to God's mercy. And history itself was changed because one man dared to say: *"Atah Ha'ish. You are the man."*

That's the mark of a game-changing man. He's not focused on guarding his own reputation—he shapes destinies, transforms families, and impacts nations by standing firmly on God's truth.

So here's the question: in your generation, in your circle, in your home…will you be that man?

Dear Heavenly Father,

I thank You for the example of Nathan—a man who chose obedience over fear, truth over silence, and Your approval over the approval of men. I admit, Lord, there have been too many times when I've taken the easy road of silence. Too many times I've valued comfort more than courage, and blended in when You called me to stand apart. Forgive me.

Give me Nathan's boldness. Fill me with Your Spirit so I can speak truth in love, even when it costs me, even when it risks rejection, even when it shakes the world around me. Remind me that the same Spirit that empowered Nathan empowers me today.

Make me into a game-changing man in my generation. Help me to refuse compromise, to resist culture's lies, and to stand firm when You call me to speak. In my home, in my workplace, in my friendships, and in my church—let me be a man who will not remain silent.

When fear whispers for me to stay quiet, let Your voice thunder louder: "Be strong and courageous, for I am with you." When I am tempted to hide, remind me that silence is deadly, but truth spoken in love brings life.

Lord, I want to be that man. Use my voice to spark repentance, to bring restoration, and to change lives for Your glory.

I pray this in the mighty name of Jesus, my King.
Amen.

GROUP STUDY QUESTIONS:

1. Has anyone ever confronted you with a hard truth that you didn't want to hear but needed to? How did you respond?

2. Where in our lives are we tempted to stay silent and allow sin to grow unchecked—in our own hearts, in our families, or in our culture?

3. What fears keep us from speaking truth today?

4. How does remembering that God is with us change the way we face those fears?

5. Nathan didn't stand in his own strength—he spoke in the power of God's Spirit. What does this mean for us in practical terms today?

6. What would it look like for you to be a game-changing man in your home, workplace, or church?

7. Where is God calling you right now to speak up, stand firm, or refuse to stay silent?

8. How can we, as a group, help you do this?

CHAPTER EIGHT
A GREAT BIG WEE LITTLE MAN

Most people who know me are aware that I am one half of a brother-sister ministry team. Not only do we work and minister together, but I also live with my sister. This means that we share many things, including work and household responsibilities, the house, a car, and even a television. (Thank God you can watch football online or I'd hardly ever get to see it!) Actually, I'm just joking because the truth is my sister is a pretty good sport.

Because she knows I like it, she is well-versed in Rocky movies, and she can talk football. She doesn't even object when I listen to *The Dan Patrick Show* while we're in the car. (If she's honest, she'll even admit she likes Dan and the Danettes.) Of course, there is also the flip side, where I graciously watch a lot of ridiculous, cheesy Hallmark movies and shows that she likes. I'm also fluent in *Gilmore Girls* because turn around is fair play.

Anyway, one of the shows that she watches every year is called *Chesapeake Shores*. Guaranteed by the end of summer, she has sat through every episode of this show about a family that lives along the Chesapeake Bay. (Honestly, the water scenery in this show is magnificent!)

Here's the thing: from the very first episode of *Chesapeake Shores*, it's clear that the O'Brien family has major problems. The parents had a very complicated marriage while the kids were growing up, and it had a massive effect on each child in the family.

The older children have vivid memories of the fighting and tension that prevailed in the house during their childhood. The younger children struggled with feelings of abandonment because their Mom eventually left their family, and their Dad ran away and buried himself in work to avoid everything.

Throughout the first season, we see that the now-adult kids are struggling to work through the issues of their past and lead healthy lives. For the most part, the parents don't get it. They can't understand why the kids can't move on, forget the past, and act like one big happy family. The mother often questions why she's blamed for everything and seen as the parent who left. (The answer is because she left.) The father points this out every time something comes up and blames everything on her. He sees himself as doing nothing wrong and won't take responsibility for how he treated her or the kids.

Honestly, when I watch the first season (with my sister, of course), the parents are really annoying because they are so oblivious to how their lives and their choices affected their kids.

Thankfully, their attitude doesn't carry into seasons two and three. Instead, during these seasons, the parents begin to realize that if they want to have a healthy relationship with their kids and help them lead healthy lives and experience healthy relationships with others, they will have to start accepting some responsibility.

In one particular scene, the father and son are on the father's boat. They've just fought, and the son is very emotional. The father wants to cover it up, pretend it didn't happen, and fix the boat.

The son is having none of it and keeps trying to talk about their relationship.

Rather than talking, the father tries to turn the conversation by asking if the son knows how to tie a particular kind of knot.

The son, discouraged, says, *"No"*.

The father laughs and says, *"You don't know much about boats, do you?"*

The son says, *"Well, no, no one was there to teach me."* [1]

For the first time, the father seems to understand his son's pain. He looks his son in the eye and genuinely says, *"I'm sorry."*

It was an honest and raw moment, and the son was genuinely touched by the first genuine apology he had received from his Dad.

That moment is a turning point for their family—a game-changer. From then on, you see the parents start working together to stop avoiding and blaming each other, and instead begin talking to their kids about what happened, apologizing to them, and making things right.

That decision to take responsibility for their actions and help their kids heal was game-changing for their family.

Over the summer, as I watched this episode, it became so apparent to me that this chapter needed to be included in this book. Because the truth is, there are a lot of men who are dealing with the issues of their past—not the past of what was done to them, but rather the past of the things that they did to other people

Many men have regrets about how they treated their spouses and children. They regret their choices to be selfish, absent, and angry. Some men actually abused their families, physically, sexually, or emotionally. Others cheated on their spouses.

Some men regret divorces and how they have been separated from their children. Others didn't take their child support or visitation days seriously and neglected their children. Some men were just so distant or self-absorbed that they might as well not have been there. They may be the parent who stayed, but their family still feels abandoned.

Please understand that this chapter is not meant to make you feel bad or condemn you. Instead, this chapter is designed to help you find a way forward—a way to be a game changer who helps those that you hurt find healing and hopefully, start building a new relationship.

This chapter is for the men who feel like the man I met one year at our Teen Challenge Mantour. As I was watching this television program, it reminded me of a conversation I had with this man after Mantour ended. He was sharing that even though he'd gone through the program and been sober for almost two years, his family (especially his kids) were struggling to rebuild the relationship.

While he was excited for what Christ was doing in his life, they still weren't sure if they could trust him. Was this just another tangent their Dad was on that would ultimately end in heartache? He admitted their fears were legitimate.

He ended by sharing that what he realized is that all he can do is continue to faithfully follow Christ and allow God to continue making him into the man he needs to be. His prayer is that with time and consistency, his family will see that the change is real and give him another chance.

The truth is, I know that this man is not alone. I know that there are men who are reading this book and asking themselves, *"How do I start to make things right?"*

How can I help the people I've hurt not only forgive me, but also actually heal and move on with their lives?

To start finding answers to this question, let's turn to the book of Luke and read about Zacchaeus.

> *Jesus entered Jericho and was passing through.*
>
> *A man was there by the name of Zacchaeus; he was a chief tax collector and was wealthy.*
>
> *He wanted to see who Jesus was, but because he was short he could not see over the crowd. So he ran ahead and climbed a sycamore-fig tree to see him, since Jesus was coming that way.*
>
> *When Jesus reached the spot, he looked up and said to him, "Zacchaeus, come down immediately. I must stay at your house today." So he came down at once and welcomed him gladly.*
>
> *All the people saw this and began to mutter, "He has gone to be the guest of a sinner."*
>
> *But Zacchaeus stood up and said to the Lord, "Look, Lord! Here and now I give half of my possessions to the poor, and if I have cheated anybody out of anything, I will pay back four times the amount."*
>
> *Jesus said to him, "Today salvation has come to this house, because this man, too, is a son of Abraham. For the Son of Man came to seek and to save the lost." -Luke 19:1-10 (NIV)*

"*Zacchaeus was a wee little man and a wee little man was he.*" (I hope those lyrics aren't copywritten, because they are the first thing that pops into my head when I read this story.

However, this is just the physical description of Zacchaeus. When we look beyond his appearance, we see a man who has made a lot of mistakes and hurt a lot of people.

He stole, he deceived, and he betrayed his country when he became a tax collector. This was a man who had many regrets.

And yet, when he heard that Jesus had come to town, he knew he had to see Him. Apparently, he was so moved by what Jesus had to say that he invited Him home for dinner.

> **GAME-CHANGING TRUTH**
> NO MATTER WHAT YOU'VE DONE OR THE TRAIL OF DAMAGE YOU'VE LEFT BEHIND, JESUS WILL FORGIVE A TRULY REPENTANT PERSON, OFFER THEM SALVATION, AND THE OPPORTUNITY TO START LIFE OVER AGAIN.

Of course, this upset the people of the town because they didn't care for Zacchaeus. Truth be told, they were probably some of the people he stole from and cheated.

Still, Jesus went.

Because no matter what you've done or the trail of damage you've left behind, Jesus will forgive a truly repentant person, offer them salvation, and the opportunity to start life over again.

As Jesus said previously, when He was eating with another tax collector, **"It is not the healthy who need a doctor, but the sick. I have not come to call the righteous, but sinners." -Mark 2:17 (NIV)**

This is a game-changing truth for anyone who has regrets for the sins and choices of their past.

However, it's important to notice that Zacchaeus' interaction with Jesus didn't end there. Instead, Zacchaeus was so inspired by Jesus and His forgiveness that he decided to make some pretty big changes in his life.

> ***But Zacchaeus stood up and said to the Lord, "Look, Lord! Here and now I give half of my possessions to the poor, and if I have cheated anybody out of anything, I will pay back four times the amount." -Luke 19:8 (NIV)***

Zacchaues was making some pretty big changes! He was a great big wee little man when it came to repenting.

This is the first step to overcoming the regrets in your life: you must make your own commitment to change, regardless of the results.

You have to want to change more than you want your next breath and commit to doing the work necessary to make the change happen.

Of course, it all begins by coming to Jesus and asking Him to forgive you of your sins and turning your life over to Him. Submitting your life to Christ is a crucial and essential step.

However, it doesn't end there. Saying a sinner's prayer doesn't make things magically change.

It's the starting point, not the finish line.

The next step is to commit to spending time with God every day, allowing you to build a personal relationship with Him.

You need to faithfully be in God's Word, reading and studying it so that you can see the changes God wants to make in your life.

As the Holy Spirit convicts you of sin or shows you areas where you need to change, you need to do whatever is necessary—everything—to make the changes.

For some, it will mean stopping drinking or doing drugs.

For others, it means dealing with their issues of anger or pornography.

Some may be able to pray through and work through issues on their own, but for other problems, they may need to consult a Bible-believing, Spirit-filled counselor. There's no shame in this—it's part of doing whatever it takes to get free.

Some individuals may benefit from a support group like *Celebrate Recovery.*

Odds are that you will need an accountability partner.

All of these are essential steps in transforming your life, letting go of your old ways, and becoming the man God wants you to be.

That is the first step—committing to change.

However, the fact is that just as Zacchaeus' sins and choices affected others, your actions also impact the people around you. That's why, like Zacchaeus, you need to do more than make things right with God. You need to do what you can to make things right with others.

The first step in this process is what the father in *Chesapeake Shores* had to do: honestly and humbly apologize to those you hurt.

You need to ask those you have hurt to forgive you humbly. Go to them and admit you were wrong without expecting anything in return.

Don't make excuses. Yes, in time, you may have the opportunity to make explanations, but this isn't the time. You want to begin by taking responsibility, saying, *"I was wrong, I am so sorry for what I did to you, will you please forgive me?".*

Remember—they don't owe you anything—you owe them everything because you damaged them.

Here's something you'll need to remember: life isn't a fairy tale. Real-life people don't have writers feeding them lines. Instead, humans have emotions, feelings, and pain that might surface in response to your apology.

That's why it's essential to allow them the time and the space to process their feelings, ask questions, raise doubts, and say what they need to say. Throughout this process (which may take time), continue in an attitude of repentance and humility, understanding their perspective.

Along the way, do your part in rebuilding the relationship.

Be kind.

Show love.

Remember them on the holidays, even if they don't reciprocate.

Show up. Be consistent. Be the man you say you want to be.

If they want to see a counselor together, go with them and be honest about what you did.

Keep growing. Keep changing. Continue to prove that God has made a change in your life and that you are not going to backslide.

Pray that God changes their hearts to allow you back into their lives.

When they are ready to start rebuilding a relationship, be the man you should have been then.

Repent, change, and choose to spend the rest of your life making up for lost time.

Choose to put others above yourself.

Show kindness instead of anger.

Don't be selfish and make everything about yourself and how others should treat you; instead, focus on how you can treat others well.

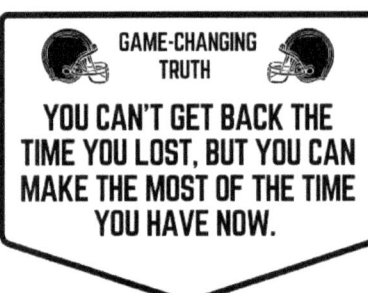

If you're given the opportunity, choose to spend time with your family even if it means you can't do what you want. Remember—you can't get back the time you lost, but you can make the most of the time you have now.

Be honest—don't make excuses, but be honest.

Also, be willing to share the family secrets. So much destruction comes because of the things that are off-limits to share. Yet, healing comes when we're open and honest, and people can truly understand.

Be willing to have the hard conversations. The odds are that the people you hurt will say things you don't want to hear, but they need to say. Be a man and have the difficult conversations. Let them share their hearts and respond with humility and grace.

More than anything else, the key to being a game-changing man is following Jesus' example and putting others above ourselves.

> *Therefore if you have any encouragement from being united with Christ, if any comfort from his love, if any common sharing in the Spirit, if any tenderness and compassion, then make my joy complete by being like-minded, having the same love, being one in spirit and of one mind. Do nothing out of selfish ambition or vain conceit. Rather, in humility value others above yourselves,*

not looking to your own interests but each of you to the interests of the others.

In your relationships with one another, have the same mindset as Christ Jesus. -Philippians 2:1-5 (NIV)

Like the Apostle Paul, forgive yourself, but don't forget. Instead, let the memory fill you with such gratitude that you spend the rest of your life serving the God Who changed you and the people that you hurt. Never take the ones around you for granted.

Be like Paul, who said, *"I was the chief of sinners, but God saved me. Now I'll live the rest of my life bringing Him glory."* (1 Timothy 1:15)

The truth is that you can't turn back the clock, but you can use every minute you have today to bring honor and glory to Jesus, to heal those you've hurt, and to build new relationships. You can be a game-changer.

Dear Heavenly Father,

I come before You humbled, aware of the mistakes I've made and the people I've hurt along the way. I confess that there have been times when I was selfish, absent, or blind to the pain I caused my family and others. I know I can't undo the past, and I know that some wounds may never fully heal—but I pray for Your guidance to step forward with honesty, humility, and a heart ready to make things right. Teach me to take responsibility for my actions, to apologize sincerely, and to show consistent love through my words and deeds. Help me to be patient with those I've hurt, understanding that forgiveness and trust take time, and that my role is to remain faithful, repentant, and committed to change.

Lord, I also pray that You transform my heart so that I become a man who mirrors Your love and grace. Let my actions reflect the humility and service of Jesus, putting others above myself and seeking to restore relationships with care, honesty, and integrity. Give me wisdom to navigate the hard conversations, courage to share the truth, and perseverance to continually prove that the change You've worked in me is real.

May my life honor You in every choice, bringing healing to my family, peace to my heart, and glory to Your name. I trust You, Lord, to work in and through me to be a true game-changer for Your kingdom and for the people I love. In Jesus' Name, Amen.

GROUP STUDY QUESTIONS:

1. How have the choices you've made in the past affected your relationships, especially with family? Are there areas where you need to take responsibility, like the father in *Chesapeake Shores*?

2. Why is a sincere, humble apology important in restoring relationships? How does it differ from making excuses or expecting forgiveness?

3. What can we learn from Zacchaeus about repentance and making things right with others? How does his response to Jesus challenge or inspire you?

4. Beyond saying *"I'm sorry,"* what practical steps can we take to show consistent change and rebuild trust in our relationships?

5. Philippians 2:1-5 calls us to value others above ourselves. How can we apply this mindset in our family, at work, and in our friendships to be *"game-changers"*?

6. How can we give others the time and space to process their pain while we continue to live in humility and repentance? What role does patience play in healing damaged relationships?

7. After reading this chapter, what is one thing you will put into practice or one thing you will change in your life?

8. How can we, as a group, help you do this?

CHAPTER NINE
THE UNKNOWN MVP'S

The NFL is a multi-billion-dollar industry. Each week, the stadiums are packed with fans watching the teams play and fight for victory. Fans cheer for, or conversely boo and scream at, the players, coaches, and officials. These are the people most fans think about being involved in a football game.

But do you ever stop and think about all the skilled workers it takes to have a game on that field?

Each stadium has a grounds crew responsible for keeping the field in top-notch condition, ensuring that players are not injured due to poor field conditions. Some people paint the lines on the field and the names on the end zone. Other workers supply the uniforms and put everything in the locker room. Hard-working individuals man concession stands. There are even maintenance men working to ensure that the 30,000-plus people using the toilets don't overload the sewage system.

We rarely think about these people, but they make the games possible, and without them, it would be disastrous. They are everyday people, doing their best with the skills they've developed to make the game and teams they love a success. They are game-changers who make the game possible.

When we think of game-changing men in the Bible, our minds often go to warriors, apostles, or prophets—men who stood boldly before nations or armies. But one of the most significant game-changers in Scripture never led an army, ruled a kingdom, or preached a fiery sermon. His name was Bezalel, and God used him in a way that reminds us that skill and hard work are as much a part of God's plan as courage and leadership.

We see Bezalel's name pop up in Exodus 31. God speaks to Moses, telling him all the things that must be built, carved, and crafted for the holy tabernacle. Moses is obviously not a builder or craftsman; he is called to lead this nation and to be their judge and chief communicator with God. He didn't have the time or ability to build all this stuff God wanted built. Thankfully, God already knew this and had a plan all set.

> *The Lord said to Moses, "See, I have called by name Bezalel the son of Uri, son of Hur, of the tribe of Judah, and I have filled him with the Spirit of God, with ability and intelligence, with knowledge and all craftsmanship, to devise artistic designs, to work in gold, silver, and bronze, in cutting stones for setting, and in carving wood, to work in every craft." -Exodus 31:1-5 (ESV).*

Think about that for a moment. God filled Bezalel with His Spirit —not to lead a nation, but to design and build. His assignment was to construct the tabernacle, the place where God's presence would dwell among His people. Every detail mattered. Every stitch, carving, and piece of furniture would reflect the glory of God.

This shows us something powerful: God values creativity just as much as He values boldness. He gifts men differently, but every gift is for His glory.

It is easy to think that to be a game-changing man, you must be a pastor, or a leader, or a great evangelist. But this isn't true. Every man can be a game-changing man that God uses for His glory. God can use whatever your skill is in life to advance His kingdom.

GAME-CHANGING TRUTH

GOD VALUES CREATIVITY JUST AS MUCH AS HE VALUES BOLDNESS. HE GIFTS MEN DIFFERENTLY, BUT EVERY GIFT IS FOR HIS GLORY.

Let's look at what God said about Bezalel again.

> *I have filled him with the Spirit of God, with ability and intelligence, with knowledge and all craftsmanship,*
> *-Exodus 31:3, ESV*

Bezalel was filled with the Spirit of God and empowered to do the work God had called him to. He wasn't simply *"naturally talented."* His skill, wisdom, and understanding were Spirit-given, Spirit-shaped, and Spirit-directed.

GAME-CHANGING TRUTH

HE WANTS TO EMPOWER WHAT YOU DO, USING THE SKILLS YOU HAVE, WHETHER YOU THINK THEY'RE GREAT OR SMALL, FOR HIS GLORY AND THE GROWTH OF HIS KINGDOM.

Guys, God wants to do the same in you. He wants to empower what you do, using the skills you have, whether you think they're great or small, for His glory and the growth of His Kingdom.

Here's what's interesting: Bezalel wasn't told just to do his best in some vague, half-hearted way. God equipped him for excellence. The tabernacle wasn't something thrown together carelessly. It was meant to be the place where God's presence would dwell, so it needed to be beautiful, crafted with care, and precise. God cared about the details because they reflected His own excellence and holiness.

Game-changing men understand this. They refuse to cut corners. They won't settle for mediocrity. They don't measure themselves by *"good enough."* Instead, they aim for excellence in every part of life, not just because they're perfectionists, but because excellence reflects the character of God. Whether they are at work, coaching their children's sports teams, building something with their hands, leading a project, or managing a household responsibility, they do it with care, effort, and intention. Why? Because everything they do is a chance to reflect the God Who made them.

Men who genuinely make a difference understand that their abilities, talents, and creativity weren't meant just for personal gain. The world tells us to use our gifts to build our own reputation, brand, and success. But God says our gifts are for His purposes. The creativity He's given you is meant to bless others, honor Him, and create something that lasts forever.

Think about it—without Bezalel, the tabernacle doesn't exist. Without the tabernacle, Israel lacks a central place of worship. Without worship, the people would drift from God. When people drift away from God, they would compromise. Their compromise would lead to sin, and this sin would lead to God's judgment. What Bezalel built mattered, not because it put his name in lights, but because it created a place for God's glory to dwell among His people and for God's people to worship God as His chosen people.

In the same way, your gifts may not look like someone else's, but they are essential. Perhaps you're not the preacher on Sunday. Maybe you don't stand behind the pulpit, lead worship, or deliver sermons. That doesn't mean your contribution is any less significant. God has placed talents, skills, and abilities in your hands that are just as vital to the work of His kingdom. You can still help the ministry flourish.

For instance, I remember in 2019, God gave us a vision to convert our two-car garage into office space for the ministry. We followed His lead and hired a contractor to do the work. We had limited funds for the project, so we could only hire the contractor to do the major rebuilding work. All the finishing work fell on us, and much of it we didn't know how to do.

Then, a church that regularly attended Mantours stepped up. Some of the men in the church were contractors, and they brought a group of men and provided us with two days of free labor. They backed their contractor trailer up, unloaded their tools, and completed all the trim work. They also built our custom room-length desk, installed a screen door, and undertook many other projects. Because of their help, we were able to complete the office, and it was finished just in time for the COVID shutdown, so we had an office to work from while we were stuck at home.

These men used their skills to build God's kingdom, enabling us to fulfill God's calling.

Perhaps you could mow the lawns so the church grounds are well-maintained and inviting. Maybe you help maintain the building, fixing what's broken or keeping everything in order.

Perhaps you keep the vans running so people can attend church, events, or outreach trips. Maybe you organize volunteers, manage schedules, create systems, or even cook meals for those in need. Every skill you have—no matter how ordinary it may seem—is a tool God can use to grow His kingdom.

Excellence isn't limited to those in the spotlight. Sometimes the men who make the most significant impact are working quietly, faithfully, and skillfully in ways no one notices—but God sees. Your hands, your mind, your energy, your problem-solving, your creativity, your organization—they all matter. Every task done with care and intention points to the glory of God.

Imagine the church as a body. The preacher might be the mouth, but every part—hands, feet, eyes, and heart—has its own role. If any one part doesn't do its part, the body can't work as it should. Your gifts, whatever they may be, are crucial to the ministry's health, growth, and impact.

So don't sell yourself short. Don't think your contribution is minor because it's behind the scenes. God can use whatever you're good at—mowing lawns, maintaining buildings, keeping vans running, managing systems, mentoring others, or offering encouragement—to expand His Kingdom. Embrace your gifts with devotion, humility, and bravery. Remember, the ministry thrives not just because of one individual, but because men and women come together, using their unique talents to honor and glorify God.

GAME-CHANGING TRUTH

GAME-CHANGING MEN TAKE WHAT GOD HAS PLACED IN THEIR HANDS AND PUT IT TO WORK FOR KINGDOM IMPACT.

Don't bury your gift. Don't despise it. Don't underestimate it. Develop it. Offer it. Use it boldly and humbly for the Lord. Game-changing men take what God has placed in their hands and put it to work for kingdom impact.

Guys, your skills matter. What you do matters. God placed those gifts in you on purpose. So let me ask you:

Where has God uniquely gifted you?

Are you using those gifts for His glory, or are you using them only for personal gain?

What's one area of your life right now where you can choose excellence instead of mediocrity?

Bezalel reminds us of a powerful truth: God doesn't only call warriors and kings—He also calls builders, craftsmen, designers, and creators. A game-changing man doesn't just fight battles; he uses his God-given skills to create, build, and serve in ways that point people back to Him.

Your gifts are not an accident. Your skill is not random. It is the Spirit of God working in you. So whatever you build, don't just build for yourself. Build in a way that strengthens God's kingdom and serves His people.

Dear Heavenly Father,

Thank You for reminding me today that You're the One Who gives me skill, wisdom, and creativity. Thank You for the gifts You've placed in my hands, even the ones I sometimes overlook or underestimate. Forgive me for the times I've used my abilities only for myself instead of for Your glory. Lord, just as You filled Bezalel with Your Spirit to build what mattered most, I ask You to fill me and shape my work so that it honors You.

Father, I don't want to squander what You've given me. Teach me to use my gifts with excellence, humility, and faithfulness, not for praise, but to point people back to You. Whether I'm in the spotlight or working behind the scenes, may my life and work create space for others to see Your presence and worship You. May everything I build—whether in my family, my work, or my community—stand as a testimony to Your greatness and glory. In Jesus' name, Amen.

GAME CHANGERS

GROUP STUDY QUESTIONS

1. When you think of a *"game-changing man"* in the Bible, who comes to mind first—and why? How does Bezalel's story challenge or expand that picture?

2. Exodus 31 states that God filled Bezalel with His Spirit to give him the skill and wisdom necessary for building. What does this tell us about where our talents and abilities truly come from?

3. What is one skill, talent, or ability God has given you?

4. Do you tend to see your work (career, family responsibilities, hobbies, or service) as just ordinary tasks, or as opportunities to glorify God? What might change if you viewed them as kingdom work?

5. What's an area of your life where you've been tempted to settle for good enough?

6. What would it look like to pursue excellence in that area as an act of worship to God?

7. How can your skills—big or small—be used to grow God's kingdom right now?

8. What is one specific step you could take this week to use your gifts in service to others?

9. How can we, as a group, help you do this?

CHAPTER TEN
BLITZED FROM WITHIN

Do you ever think that sometimes we are a little too hard on the people in the Bible? Sometimes I wonder if we, sitting in our comfortable twenty-first-century *'we-know-the-end-of-the-story'* mindset, don't tend to minimize some of the situations the great men and women of the Bible faced.

Take, for instance, the verses where God tells Joshua to be strong and courageous.

> *After the death of Moses the servant of the Lord, the Lord said to Joshua son of Nun, Moses' aide: "Moses my servant is dead. Now then, you and all these people, get ready to cross the Jordan River into the land I am about to give to them—to the Israelites. I will give you every place where you set your foot, as I promised Moses. Your territory will extend from the desert to Lebanon, and from the great river, the Euphrates—all the Hittite country—to the*

> *Mediterranean Sea in the west. No one will be able to stand against you all the days of your life. As I was with Moses, so I will be with you; I will never leave you nor forsake you.*
>
> *Be strong and courageous, because you will lead these people to inherit the land I swore to their ancestors to give them. -Joshua 1:1-6 (NIV)*

It's easy to read these verses and think, *"Come on, Joshua, what's your problem? I mean, man up, dude! God told you to be strong and courageous. He said you'd inherit the Promised Land. He promised He'd be with you like He was with Moses. What are you afraid of? Stop being a baby, be strong and courageous, and do what God wants you to do!"*

We can think these things because we know the end of the story. However, it's important to remember that when God gave Joshua these commands, Joshua didn't know the outcome. At this point, he couldn't even imagine the walls of Jericho crumbling, how Israel's enemies' hearts melted with fear, and how God miraculously intervened and literally gave His people the Promised Land.

Here's what Joshua did know:

First, Moses was dead, and Joshua was the new leader. For the first time in his life, all of the responsibility for their lives rested on him. Think about that for a moment.

Having served as Moses' assistant for years, Joshua was familiar with the people he was leading and their history. He knew they'd been through a few battles, but they weren't warriors. He may have wondered if they were up for the task.

After all, the Israelites weren't known for their faith and obedience to God. Instead, they were prone to fear, complaining, turning away from God's will, and disobeying God's commands. He'd seen them do some wild things when they were unhappy with their leaders, including threatening to stone them.

Joshua probably still remembered the day when he and Caleb returned with the other ten spies that Moses sent to spy out the land they were about to attack. When Joshua and Caleb went against the advice of the other ten spies and encouraged the people, saying, "*With God's help, we can do it!*", the people tried to stone them. (Numbers 14)

Not a great day. Now it was time to lead these people's children into the Promised Land. What would they do when the going got tough?

Then there were the enemies Joshua was facing. Here's the thing: even though the spies who discouraged the people from entering the Promised Land years ago didn't trust God, they weren't entirely wrong in their report.

Joshua had been in the Promised Land, and he knew the spies' description of the land was accurate. (Numbers 13:26-33)

There was no doubt—the city-states in central, southern, and northern Canaan were well-armed, protected, and impressive.[1] This was especially true of Jericho, where the walls surrounding the city may have been as high as thirty feet and twenty feet thick.[2] And Jericho was the first city they had to conquer!

This brings us to another reason why Joshua may have been struggling with courage: Just because God said He would give the Israelites their Promised Land, Joshua didn't know HOW God was going to do it.

Remember, this is before God used Joshua to part the Red Sea (Joshua 3), before they heard the report that everyone was afraid of them (Joshua 2:9-11), and before the walls of Jericho fell (Joshua 6).

At this point, Joshua had no idea what would happen as he prepared to follow God in faith. He only knew that God was calling him to step up, lead the people into battle, and trust that God had a plan to give them victory.

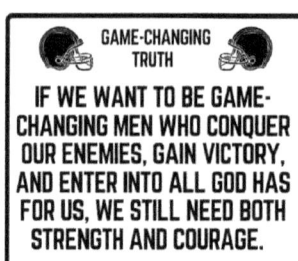

GAME-CHANGING TRUTH
IF WE WANT TO BE GAME-CHANGING MEN WHO CONQUER OUR ENEMIES, GAIN VICTORY, AND ENTER INTO ALL GOD HAS FOR US, WE STILL NEED BOTH STRENGTH AND COURAGE.

Not much has changed today. If we want to be game-changing men who conquer our enemies, gain victory, and enter into all God has for us, we still need both strength and courage.

Let's not pretend that we aren't all facing enemies and fighting in a battle. Just because our enemies aren't coming at us with swords and spears like Joshua's doesn't make them any less intimidating or difficult to conquer.

The fact is that as men of God, we are all in a spiritual battle.

> *Finally, be strong in the Lord and in his mighty power. Put on the full armor of God, so that you can take your stand against the devil's schemes. For our struggle is not against flesh and blood, but against the rulers, against the authorities, against the powers of this dark world and against the spiritual forces of evil in the heavenly realms.*
> *-Ephesians 6:10-12 (NIV)*

While Joshua was fighting physical armies, the battlefield where we wage our war is often within our own minds. Often, the enemy we need to drive out is the sin and idolatry in our lives.

It's interesting that, just as God told Joshua to be *"strong and courageous"*, we are encouraged to *"be strong"* in our spiritual battle. Because here's the thing—following God when the Holy Spirit leads you to fight the spiritual enemies in your life takes an enormous amount of strength and courage.

In fact, one of the bravest prayers you will ever pray is, *"Search me, O God, and know my heart. Try me and know my thoughts! And see if there be any grievous way in me, and lead me in the way everlasting!"* -Psalm 139:23-24 (ESV)

It's a pretty game-changing prayer: *"Dear God, please show me if there is anything in my life that grieves You. Do whatever You need to do to reveal hidden sin—in action and in thought—so that I can repent and change and walk in Your plan for my life."*

Talk about strength and courage!!

A man truly committed to experiencing God's whole plan and fulfilling His purpose will sincerely pray this prayer, genuinely mean it, and actively pursue victory in areas where the Holy Spirit highlights.

> **GAME-CHANGING TRUTH**
> A MAN TRULY COMMITTED TO EXPERIENCING GOD'S WHOLE PLAN AND FULFILLING HIS PURPOSE WILL SINCERELY PRAY THIS PRAYER, GENUINELY MEAN IT, AND ACTIVELY PURSUE VICTORY IN AREAS WHERE THE HOLY SPIRIT HIGHLIGHTS.

"How will I know which areas the Holy Spirit wants to address?"

Trust me, the Holy Spirit will let you know.

Sometimes, it will be during your time of prayer when the Holy Spirit speaks to your heart and reveals something that needs to change. At other times, you may be reading your Bible and a verse jumps out at you, telling you a sin in your life that needs to be addressed. It can happen while you're listening to a sermon or even a song. I've even been convicted of sin while I was watching television!

The specific place or time doesn't matter; what matters is that the Holy Spirit uses something to communicate with your heart, saying, *"This needs to change."*

For instance, I remember one night I was watching television when my Dad walked into the room. To be honest, I was watching a popular television show that was both very funny and off-color.

When my Dad walked in, I turned off the television, because with his history, I didn't want him watching it. That very moment, the Holy Spirit said, *"If you don't want your Dad watching it, why are you?"*

Like an arrow hitting a bullseye, I felt the conviction of the Holy Spirit point out that I was compromising and sinning. So I asked God to forgive me, and I haven't watched that show again.

That's the response a game-changing man of God needs to have anytime the Holy Spirit convicts him of sin.

First, we need to repent honestly—go to God in prayer and sincerely ask Him to forgive us for our sin.

Then, we should complete the process of repentance by turning away from our wrongdoings and stop sinning. We must do everything in our power to eliminate sin from our lives and never repeat it.

Now I know there are some of you out there saying, *"Cute story, Jamie, but the sin I'm dealing with is a little bigger than watching a PG-13 show on television. I've been to the altar and repented lots of times, but I'm still struggling to defeat this enemy and overcome."*

First of all, I want you to know that you are not alone. We've all experienced this at some point in our lives. I decided to include this chapter because I know how tough it can be to deal with sin and struggles that have formed a stronghold in your life. But just because it's difficult doesn't mean you have to stay trapped and entangled.

Through the power of the Holy Spirit and your determination to partner with Him and do all that you can to overcome, you can gain the victory. Just like Joshua defeated the well-fortified cities and drove his enemies out of the Promised Land, you can defeat the enemies that are keeping you in bondage in your life.

How do you do it?

It begins by having the strength and the courage to admit there is a problem.

Before you can defeat an enemy, you must admit that it exists and that it is actually an enemy and not a friend.

This takes courage. The truth is, when the Holy Spirit highlights an area He wants to work on in our lives, our first response is often one of resistance. We either think, *"This can't be true,"* or we admit, *"Okay, it's true,"* but quickly downplay it with, *"Is it really that big of a deal?"*

And yet, true freedom and healing cannot come until we move beyond denial and have the strength and courage to say, "I realize this is a problem in my life, and I want to overcome it. I don't want it to control or hurt me anymore."

When you reach a point where you say, "I want freedom, deliverance, and healing more than I want my next breath," now you're ready to fight and overcome.

This is true regardless of the battle you face. Whether it be overcoming anger, abuse, sexual addiction, drinking, lying, false teaching, or any other sin or issue, Alcoholics Anonymous has it right: It all starts with overcoming denial and admitting you have a problem.

Okay, so you admit that the Holy Spirit is right and you need to overcome this issue. Now what?

Now, you need to have the courage to allow Him to reveal the root of the problem.

How does this happen?

When our hearts are right, the Holy Spirit can reveal to us the true cause of the problems that control us.

Most strongholds are the result of one of four things:

- Unconfessed sin in your life.

- Our Experiences—Unresolved issues from your past—either things you've done or things that were done to you, and how they make us view the world.

- The World We Were Born Into-Our Parents

- False Teaching[3]

Strongholds can originate from any of these factors or be a combination of them. Either way, the same truth applies: you must identify the root of the problem so that you can eradicate it from your life.

Once again, this requires incredible strength and courage, as it's scary to take the necessary steps to open the Pandora's box of the past without knowing exactly what you will find. In fact, one of the main reasons many won't partner with the Holy Spirit to overcome the issues causing their problems is that they don't want to face the truth.

They don't want to remember the past or relive the pain.

They don't want to face the truth they buried, especially if it was traumatic or painful.

Some people don't want to deal with the facts about a person close to them and look at them for who they really are, rather than the rose-colored picture they painted to cover up the heartache.

There are many reasons why people want to keep the past and the root causes of their issues locked away. However, the truth is that as long as you keep it locked up and hidden away, it will have control over you. When you face your fear and say, *"I want to get to the root of this issue,"* you are in control. That is the first step to freedom.

Now, I'm not going to sugarcoat this and say it is going to be easy. The truth is that uncovering the root cause of the issue can be extremely painful. You may not like what you see there about others or yourself. People bury painful things for a reason. You will discover things about yourself that you didn't know before.

GAME-CHANGING TRUTH

WHEN YOU FACE YOUR FEAR AND SAY, "I WANT TO GET TO THE ROOT OF THIS ISSUE," YOU ARE IN CONTROL. THAT IS THE FIRST STEP TO FREEDOM.

While the truth can be painful, it is ultimately what frees us. To become game-changing men walking in freedom and victory, we must have the courage to confront the truth, release its grip on us, and let the Holy Spirit heal and liberate us.

What happens next?

So, you've acknowledged there's a problem and allowed the Holy Spirit to reveal the root cause. You've been strong and courageous, facing the pain. Like puss leaving a wound, remembering released the pain. (Gross, I know, but true.)

Now it's time to start the process of healing and walking in freedom.

During this time, it's essential to prioritize spending time with God—not interceding for the whole world, but talking to Him about what's going on inside of you. Share your heart openly and honestly. Don't be surprised if He speaks words of Scripture or comforts you back. Remember: God wants you to heal and be free. He's pulling for you and will do all He can to help as you spend time with Him.

It's also essential that, as you're healing, you prioritize time in God's Word.

Why?

God's Word will help you see how to move forward. The truth is that your life will be very different as you live without the pain in your heart. God's Word can show you how to rebuild your life.

Here are some other courageous steps you can take to overcome and find freedom:

- Talk to someone—a godly friend, your pastor, a mentor, or an accountability partner about what the Holy Spirit is doing in your life. I promise you that the more you talk, the more freedom you will find.

- Try journaling. I know this sounds girly, but it isn't. It's just a way to get the pain out of your heart and onto paper. If writing doesn't work for you, try typing or talking to a computer. The point isn't to write a book—it's to set yourself free.

- Make a list of practical changes you need to make in your life. Remember, this whole thing began because you asked the Holy Spirit to search your heart and show you what He wanted to change. Now, let's create a plan for how to begin the change.

- If you are struggling with an addiction, consider joining a *Celebrate Recovery* group or seeking out treatment from a Christian, Spirit-filled treatment center.

- Consider consulting a Bible-believing, Spirit-filled counselor who can help you identify the root causes of your issue and develop practical steps to move forward.

Here's an important truth: Asking for help to overcome sin, addiction, or trauma in your life is not a sign of weakness. It isn't unmasculine or wimpy.

It is literally being strong and courageous.

It's being man enough to say, *"I do not want my enemies to defeat me for the rest of my life. I don't want these things to affect me, my family, or the people in my life. I'm sick of it, so I am going to go to war with them. I'm going to do whatever it takes to follow Joshua's example, be strong and courageous, and remove my enemies from my life."*

The man who makes this decision isn't a wimp—he's a warrior—willing to do whatever it takes to be a game-changer in his own life and the world around him.

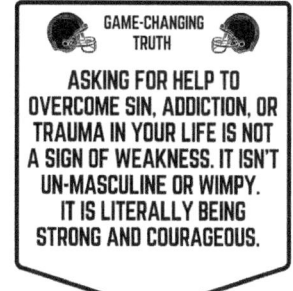

GAME-CHANGING TRUTH

ASKING FOR HELP TO OVERCOME SIN, ADDICTION, OR TRAUMA IN YOUR LIFE IS NOT A SIGN OF WEAKNESS. IT ISN'T UN-MASCULINE OR WIMPY. IT IS LITERALLY BEING STRONG AND COURAGEOUS.

Are you that man?

Are you ready to be strong and courageous and gain victory?

Start today by asking the Holy Spirit to search your heart and show you what He wants to address. Then, have the courage, strength, and determination to face it head-on and overcome in victory.

Dear Heavenly Father,

I admit that fear often tries to take hold of me. I like to think I'm strong, but the truth is, there are moments when I feel weak, overwhelmed, or unsure of what to do next. Forgive me for the times I've let fear, doubt, or insecurity keep me from obeying You fully. I know You call me to be strong and courageous, not because of my own abilities, but because You are with me.

Lord, I need Your strength in my daily battles—the temptations I face, the pressures of life, the responsibilities that weigh on me. Give me the courage to take the next step in faith, even when I can't see the outcome. Remind me that I don't fight alone, that You never leave me and never forsake me. Fill me with Your Spirit so I can walk boldly, love deeply, and live faithfully. Make me a man who draws his courage from Your presence and his strength from Your promises.

In Jesus' Amen.

GROUP STUDY QUESTIONS:

1. What personal battles or struggles do you find the hardest to overcome, and why do they seem so difficult?

2. How does fear, guilt, or shame keep us stuck in cycles we want to break free from?

3. In what ways does God's promise never to leave us give hope when we feel like our issues are too big to handle?

4. What practical steps have helped you (or could help you) rely on God instead of trying to fight your battles in your own strength?

5. How can being honest about our weaknesses with trusted friends or mentors help us overcome them?

6. After reading this chapter, what is one thing you will put into practice or one thing you will change in your life?

7. How can we, as a group, help you do this?

CHAPTER ELEVEN
CHAMPIONS DON'T PLAY ALONE

I love a good sports movie, especially those based on football. They can make you laugh, get you fired up, or leave you staring at the screen, wondering how in *The Game Plan* Dwayne *"The Rock"* Johnson, clearly too ripped to ever throw a football, somehow manages to pull it off. *The Waterboy* will have you roaring and yelling, *"You can do it,"* for weeks after watching.[1] *Remember The Titans* will make you suddenly feel like you should be running drills in your driveway—even if you haven't touched a football since middle school. But *Brian's Song*? That's a different beast.

They say real men don't cry. Apparently, *"they"* have never seen men watch *Brian's Song*. Suddenly, the locker room, the football field, and a 1970s bromance are enough to turn the toughest guy into a sniffling, popcorn-choking mess. It sneaks up, taps you on the shoulder, and whispers, *"Bro... friendships matter."* And just like that, you're ugly-crying over two guys being best friends and wondering why no one ever taught you how to be that kind of friend.

Well, wonder no more, because that is what we are going to look at in this chapter: how to develop game-changing friendships. Let's explore one of my favorite men in the Bible to illustrate this... Jonathan.

I absolutely love Jonathan. There is so much we can learn from this man. He shows us how to be a man who boldly faces the enemy instead of cowering in fear and hiding (1 Samuel 14). He shows us how to overcome cruel words spoken into our lives (1 Samuel 20:30-31). He shows us how to break generational patterns and not turn out like the father who raised us. However, the thing he is most remembered for is being a good friend. We can all learn from Jonathan!

Men, we all need friends in our lives. Unfortunately, now more than ever, men are living their lives friendless and isolated.

Check out these stats from the *Survey Center for American Life*.

"Thirty years ago, a majority of men (55 percent) reported having at least six close friends. Today, that number has been cut in half. Slightly more than one in four (27 percent) men have six or more close friends today. Fifteen percent of men have no close friendships at all, a fivefold increase since 1990."[2]

Another survey by a men's health charity has even more dire numbers. *Movember Foundation* reveals that *"27% of those surveyed did not have any close friends or any friends at all."*[3]

That is one in four men! That is devastating!

The survey goes on to say this: *"Nearly half (47%) of men feel they are unable to confide in friends about their problems. This survey also found men aren't creating opportunities to meet up with their friends, for example; nearly two in five never go out for food (38%) with their close friends. Furthermore, when it comes to life challenges, only one in ten (10%) men turn to family and friends for help when facing a challenge in life.* [3]

Staggering numbers! It's no wonder that so many men feel isolated and alone. If the world ever needed game-changing men like Jonathan who demonstrate friendship, it is now. Let's look at his life.

We talked earlier about how David had stood in the gap when everyone else cowered when he stood up and defeated Goliath the Giant. For his victory, David was awarded riches, the king's daughter as a wife, and his family lived tax-free (1 Samuel 17:25). But more importantly, David received a true friend. We read that after his victory, he met Jonathan, and they instantly became friends.

> **As soon as he had finished speaking to Saul, the soul of Jonathan was knit to the soul of David, and Jonathan loved him as his own soul. And Saul took him that day and would not let him return to his father's house. Then Jonathan made a covenant with David, because he loved him as his own soul. -1 Samuel 18:1–3 (ESV)**

Here, we see the depth of Jonathan's loyalty. He loved David selflessly, without jealousy, even though David's rise threatened his own claim to the throne. True friendship, like Jonathan's, isn't founded on convenience or selfish motives. Instead, it's rooted in sincere love, dedication, and a readiness to rejoice in another's achievements, even when they pose a challenge to our own comfort or ambitions.

Jonathan also exemplifies courage in protecting his friend. After David defeated Goliath, the women in the streets began to sing **"Saul has slain thousands, and David tens of thousands"** in celebration of the victory. (1 Samuel 18:7) This didn't sit well with Saul. The man, already known for his moods and dark spirits from time to time, completely lost his marbles and became consumed by jealousy and rage. He decided he needed to kill David before David took away his kingdom.

Saul told Jonathan and his trusted men about his plan to kill David. Jonathan quickly warns David, and then goes to talk to his nut job father.

> *And Jonathan spoke well of David to Saul his father and said to him, "Let not the king sin against his servant David, because he has not sinned against you, and because his deeds have brought good to you. For he took his life in his hand and he struck down the Philistine, and the Lord worked a great salvation for all Israel. You saw it, and rejoiced. Why then will you sin against innocent blood by killing David without cause?" And Saul listened to the voice of Jonathan. Saul swore, "As the Lord lives, he shall not be put to death." And Jonathan called David, and Jonathan reported to him all these things. And Jonathan brought David to Saul, and he was in his presence as before. -Samuel 19:4-7 (ESV)*

GAME-CHANGING TRUTH
BEING A GOOD FRIEND SOMETIMES MEANS SPEAKING UP AND ADVOCATING FOR SOMEONE ELSE, EVEN WHEN IT'S RISKY OR UNCOMFORTABLE.

Jonathan intervened and spared David's life for the time being. Jonathan's intervention teaches us an important lesson. Being a good friend sometimes means speaking up and advocating for someone else, even when it's risky or uncomfortable.

For a short time, Saul calmed himself. But his jealousy and paranoia about David returned, and he once again tried to kill him.

David again reaches out to Jonathan for help. Again, Jonathan agreed to find out if Saul really intended to kill David. If it was true, he agreed to help David escape.

> *"...But should it please my father to do you harm, the Lord do so to Jonathan and more also if I do not disclose it to you and send you away, that you may go in safety. May the Lord be with you, as he has been with my father. If I am still alive, show me the steadfast love of the Lord, that I may not die; and do not cut off your steadfast love from my house forever, when the Lord cuts off every one of the enemies of David from the face of the earth."*
>
> *And Jonathan made a covenant with the house of David, saying, "May the Lord take vengeance on David's enemies." And Jonathan made David swear again by his love for him, for he loved him as he loved his own soul.*
> *-1 Samuel 20:13-17 (ESV)*

One key characteristic of Jonathan's friendship was his humility. He didn't let envy damage their relationship. Jonathan knew that God had chosen David to succeed Saul as king. Usually, he would have been next in line to inherit his father's throne. But he accepted God's plan and supported David. His heart was so in tune with God that he put the new plan into action and stood by David. He didn't try to undermine David or cling to his own position. Instead, he made a covenant with David and helped him in every way.

The text repeatedly stresses that Jonathan's love for David was genuine and selfless. He could have been jealous of David's future as king, but he chose to rejoice in it and support him. We can follow Jonathan's example by celebrating others' successes, fighting jealousy, and being supportive rather than competitive in our own lives.

Jonathan once again went to speak to his father, but this time it didn't go as well.

> *Then Saul's anger was kindled against Jonathan, and he said to him, "You son of a perverse, rebellious woman, do I not know that you have chosen the son of Jesse to your own shame, and to the shame of your mother's nakedness? For as long as the son of Jesse lives on the earth, neither you nor your kingdom shall be established. Therefore send and bring him to me, for he shall surely die."*
>
> *Then Jonathan answered Saul his father, "Why should he be put to death? What has he done?"*
>
> *But Saul hurled his spear at him to strike him. So Jonathan knew that his father was determined to put David to death. And Jonathan rose from the table in fierce anger and ate no food the second day of the month, for he was grieved for David, because his father had disgraced him. -1 Samuel 20:30-34 (ESV)*

Saul, in a jealous rage, tried to kill his own son! Jonathan knew now that his Dad wouldn't rest until David was dead. So he went to David and warned him, telling him he had to run.

> *Jonathan said to David, "Go in peace, because we have sworn both of us in the name of the Lord, saying, 'The Lord shall be between me and you, and between my offspring and your offspring, forever.'" And he rose and departed, and Jonathan went into the city. -1 Samuel 20:42 (ESV)*

So David was forced to flee from Saul's wrath, leaving his friend behind. But this wasn't the end of their relationship. Years after David left, we find him feeling defeated and discouraged. The priests at Nob had all been killed because of him. He sought refuge with the Philistines, who wanted him dead, forcing David to feign insanity to survive. He constantly had to be on the run, and his rich, deep friendship with Jonathan had been replaced by friendships with down-and-out men who had lost everything and were also on the run from Saul. It's easy to see how the stress of it all left David feeling defeated and alone.

But David wasn't alone. He still had Jonathan. Even when distance, danger, and death separated them, the bond remained strong.

> *David remained in the strongholds in the wilderness, in the hill country of the wilderness of Ziph. And Saul sought him every day, but God did not give him into his hand.*
>
> *David saw that Saul had come out to seek his life. David was in the wilderness of Ziph at Horesh. And Jonathan, Saul's son, rose and went to David at Horesh, and strengthened his hand in God. And he said to him, "Do not fear, for the hand of Saul my father shall not find you. You shall be king over Israel, and I shall be next to you. Saul my father also knows this." And the two of them made a covenant before the Lord. David remained at Horesh, and Jonathan went home. -1 Samuel 23:14–18 (ESV)*

Jonathan shows us that a real friend isn't just someone who's around all the time, but someone who sticks by you no matter what. Being loyal, encouraging, and putting others first matters more than our situation.

Jonathan's friendship with David isn't just a story to admire—it's a blueprint for how we can be better friends today. His example pushes us to examine our own relationships.

Are we celebrating our friends? Are we protecting and advocating for them? Are we showing loyalty even when it's inconvenient?

Friendships like Jonathan and David's are rare, but when we cultivate them with care, courage, humility, and commitment, they don't just improve our lives—they reflect God's own heart and bring glory to Him.

As we wrap up this chapter, here are some practical steps to take to become a better friend.

1. **Talk as well as do.**

Often, we, as men, see our friends as people with whom we do things. We play fantasy football, go to dinner, play video games, or watch movies, and so on. We focus on the activity.

There is a joke I heard recently where a wife was frustrated with her husband after he came home from golfing with a friend. He told her the friend was getting divorced.

She had a million questions, such as why? Did someone cheat? How long has the marriage been in trouble? Who was getting the house? On and on she went with questions, only to have her husband answer each one with, *"I don't know."*

GAME-CHANGING TRUTH

DEEP, MEANINGFUL FRIENDSHIPS MOVE PAST FOCUSING ON THE ACTIVITY AND FOCUS ON EACH OTHER.

Flabbergasted that the husband didn't ask any of these questions, she asked what he did know, and he replied, *"I know he got a new driver."*

The point of the joke was to highlight that men often spend hours together but never discuss anything truly meaningful or important. Unfortunately, this is true. Deep, meaningful friendships move past focusing on the activity and focus on each other. Talk. Share. Ask questions. Don't distract yourself from the conversation. It's fun to do stuff with friends, but relationships grow when we engage and communicate.

2. Allow your friend to share.

Often, men don't feel comfortable sharing struggles and problems with other men. But such boundaries shouldn't exist in true friendships. We need to be willing to let our friends talk about struggles, fears, insecurities, and issues, and be there for them in their time of need. You don't have to have all the answers, but you do need to let them share their thoughts.

3. Friends can speak the truth even when the other person doesn't want to hear it.

Sometimes, the best thing a friend can do is to say what you don't want to hear but need to hear. Proverbs 27:6 says, ***"Faithful are the wounds of a friend"***. *(ESV)*

True friends tell us hard truths, correct our mistakes, or call us out on behavior that could harm us. These *"wounds"* are faithful because they are honest, caring, and intended to help us grow. True friends don't just flatter us or say only what we want to hear. That kind of empty praise may feel good 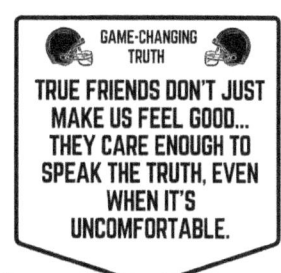 in the moment, but it doesn't help us make better choices or become stronger individuals.

This kind of correction can sting at first, but it protects you, strengthens your character, and builds a deeper level of trust between you. The key lesson is that true friends don't just make us feel good… they care enough to speak the truth, even when it's uncomfortable.

4. Real friends can rely on each other

There's nothing worse than friends who disappear when you really need them. Too often, people reveal their true nature when life becomes difficult.. If you've ever struggled and reached out for support, only to hear nothing but silence, you know exactly what I mean. True friends don't let each other down.

Being there for a friend doesn't have to be complicated. Sometimes it's as simple as sending a quick text, grabbing a slice of pizza after work, or saying, *"Let me know if you need anything."* Those small gestures show that you care and remind a guy he's not facing life alone.

Great friends step up when it counts. They show up in tangible, practical ways, proving that loyalty and presence matter more than words.

5. True friends will always encourage you to become the best man you can be, even if it means you outdo them.

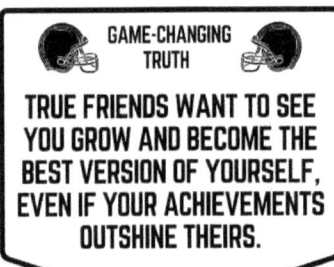

GAME-CHANGING TRUTH

TRUE FRIENDS WANT TO SEE YOU GROW AND BECOME THE BEST VERSION OF YOURSELF, EVEN IF YOUR ACHIEVEMENTS OUTSHINE THEIRS.

True friends want to see you grow and become the best version of yourself, even if your achievements outshine theirs. A real friend doesn't feel threatened or jealous when you achieve more, improve your skills, or reach goals they haven't. Instead, they celebrate your progress and push you to aim higher, challenge yourself, and reach your potential.

This kind of friendship is built on genuine care, not competition or pride. It's about supporting one another to become stronger, wiser, and better men. True friends hold you accountable, cheer you on, and inspire you to keep growing, even if it means you might outdo them in certain areas. True friends measure their loyalty by your growth and well-being, not by comparing themselves to you.

Finally, remember this.

> ***A man who has friends must himself be friendly, But there is a friend who sticks closer than a brother. -Proverbs 18:14 (NKJV)***

Developing friendships requires effort and work, but it is ultimately worth it. A game-changing man needs to be a man who has friends. This game-changing friendship has the power to change the world.

Dear Heavenly Father, I thank You for the example of Jonathan. His courage, humility, loyalty, and love show me what real friendship looks like. Lord, I confess that sometimes I have not been the friend I should be. I get busy, distracted, or even jealous, instead of celebrating the people You've placed in my life. Forgive me, Lord, and help me to grow into the kind of man who lifts others up, protects them, and encourages them to follow after You. Teach me to be bold enough to speak truth when it's needed, humble enough to celebrate others' victories, and faithful enough to stand by my friends even when it's hard.

Lord, I don't want to live isolated or alone. You created us for relationship—with You and with others. I ask You to surround me with godly friends, men who will sharpen me, challenge me, and walk with me as we pursue You together. And make me into a Jonathan for someone else, a friend who strengthens their hand in You, who points them back to Your promises when they're weary or afraid. Thank You that You are the ultimate Friend Who never leaves or forsakes me. Help me to reflect Your love in every friendship I build. In Jesus' Name, Amen.

GROUP STUDY QUESTIONS:

1. Surveys show that many men feel isolated and lack close friendships. Why do you think it's so hard for men to develop and maintain meaningful friendships in today's culture?

2. Jonathan could have been jealous of David's success, yet he chose to celebrate him and support him instead. How do you handle it when a friend succeeds in an area where you might feel left behind?

3. Jonathan risked his own safety by standing up to Saul to protect David. What are some practical ways we can stand up for or defend our friends today, even when it might cost us something?

4. Jonathan encouraged David in the middle of his discouragement and fear. Can you think of a time when a friend encouraged you at a low point? What impact did it have on you?

5. Proverbs 27:6 says, **"Faithful are the wounds of a friend."** How do you respond when a friend lovingly calls you out or challenges you? Why is this so important for spiritual growth?

6. Jonathan and David's friendship was marked by loyalty, humility, and selflessness. Which of these qualities do you most need to grow in as a friend, and what steps can you take this week to begin strengthening that area?

7. After reading this chapter, what is one thing you will put into practice or one thing you will change in your life?

8. How can we, as a group, help you do this?

CHAPTER TWELVE
BUILDING A DYNASTY

Anyone who knows me knows I love fantasy football. One of my favorite formats has become guillotine fantasy football, where every week, the lowest-scoring team is eliminated and all their players become free agents, available to be bid on and added to your team. Each week, a team is eliminated until only two teams remain. What was once a weak team made of fringe players on 18 different rosters becomes a juggernaut of two teams.

It is really fun and intense. You can lose a matchup and survive as long as you aren't the lowest scoring team, but if you are close to being the lowest scoring team, or *"OTB"* (on the bubble) as they call it, Monday Night Football gets intense as you wait to see if you get the chop. Last week, I was up late watching every play to see if I survived, begging the Chargers to stop throwing the ball to Ladd McConkey! I kept my neck by .54 points!

But where I really thrive is in dynasty leagues, where each year you have the same players and you draft rookies. I am proud to say I have won my longest-running dynasty league five of the last seven years. I love researching the rookies and building a juggernaut team.

This past season, one rookie I had my eye on was RJ Harvey, my Denver Broncos' 2nd-round pick. I was thrilled when he fell to me in the league I had been dominating, and I figuratively ran to the podium to draft him.

However, shortly after, my Broncos signed veteran running back J.K. Dobbins. I was confused. Why sign him when we took a rookie so early? More importantly, will this impact Harvey in fantasy? It made no sense to me.

However, it began to make sense when I listened to J.K. Dobbins explain his relationship with the young rookie. He said the following:

"Whenever I came in as a rookie with the Baltimore Ravens I had a Heisman Trophy winner, a guy who was well-established, in Mark Ingram. And no matter what, he would always give what was right by me. I saw that and it meant ... Mark and I are still best friends today. He was a great mentor, a great veteran. He was teaching me things that were helping me get better as a football player. That meant the world to me because at the end of the day we're all chasing a dream.

So now it's my job to help the young man get to where he needs to go because eventually I'm going to retire and when I retire I want to look back and say I really helped that kid. If he's still playing and I'm retired, I want to look and say, 'I taught him that. I told him to do that.' It's kind of like having a little brother. And it helps us win games."[1]

I LOVED THIS! This is a game-changing attitude! It is the heart of a dynasty-making man of God.

Guys, God never designed us to keep wisdom, faith, or life lessons to ourselves. We are called to receive from those who have gone before us, live it out faithfully, and then pass it on to those who will come after us. As Dobbins said, it's like having a younger brother — you walk with them, teach them, encourage them, and celebrate their victories.

As men of God, our influence multiplies when we mentor others. A game-changing man doesn't just chase his own dream—he invests in helping others achieve theirs. When we choose to pour into the next generation, we create a ripple effect that outlives us. Someday, when we're no longer *"in the game,"* we'll be able to look back with joy and say, *"I taught him that. I encouraged him in that. I helped him walk with God."*

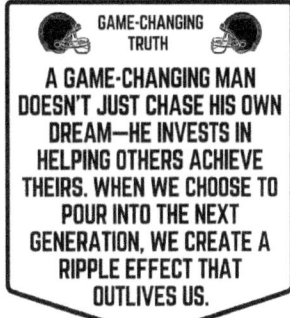

GAME-CHANGING TRUTH

A GAME-CHANGING MAN DOESN'T JUST CHASE HIS OWN DREAM—HE INVESTS IN HELPING OTHERS ACHIEVE THEIRS. WHEN WE CHOOSE TO POUR INTO THE NEXT GENERATION, WE CREATE A RIPPLE EFFECT THAT OUTLIVES US.

The Bible is full of game-changing men who adopted this same attitude.

- Moses mentored Joshua
- Eli mentored Samuel
- Samuel mentored David
- David mentored Solomon
- Elijah mentored Elisha
- Elisha mentored Gehazi
- Jehoiada mentored Joash
- Jesus mentored the Twelve Disciples
- Barnabas mentored Paul
- Paul mentored Timothy
- Paul mentored Titus

These men all saw the value of building a dynasty of game-changing men to carry the ball after they were gone. We need to do the same.

For too long, men have allowed insecurities and intimidation to stop them from raising up younger men. They feared being replaced. But that is precisely our job as men of God. Every man transitions from a player to a coach. It is natural.

A man I highly respect calls it an encourager season—where your primary calling is to cheer on, bless, and release others.

Guys, we need to stop fighting among ourselves and boasting about our successes. We can't keep holding others back to protect our own turf. Instead, let's set a good example for the next generation to follow. Cheer them on and encourage them to go even further in God's Kingdom. Then celebrate like crazy when they do!

Here's a phrase that encapsulates this attitude.

"My generation's ceiling is the next generation's floor."

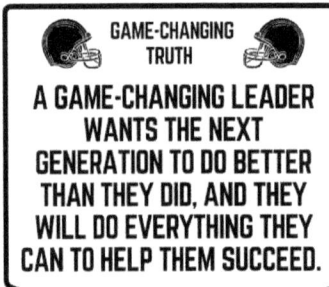

GAME-CHANGING TRUTH
A GAME-CHANGING LEADER WANTS THE NEXT GENERATION TO DO BETTER THAN THEY DID, AND THEY WILL DO EVERYTHING THEY CAN TO HELP THEM SUCCEED.

This phrase defines mentorship perfectly. Our purpose in life should be to guide the next generation so they can surpass us spiritually. We shouldn't hold them back to serve our own interests. A game-changing leader wants the next generation to do better than they did, and they will do everything they can to help them succeed.

Mentorship is more than advice—it's discipleship. When a younger man sees how you treat your family, how you honor God in your work, how you respond to temptation, or how you handle setbacks, he is learning more than a sermon could ever teach. A game-changing man doesn't just tell the next generation how to live; he shows them. He recognizes that his ceiling can become their floor, that his lessons can prevent their failures, and that his encouragement can fuel their destiny.

The reality is, the world is not shy about mentoring the next generation. Social media, celebrities, influencers, and peers continually shape the way young men think, talk, and behave. If we don't step up, someone else will. A game-changing man of God

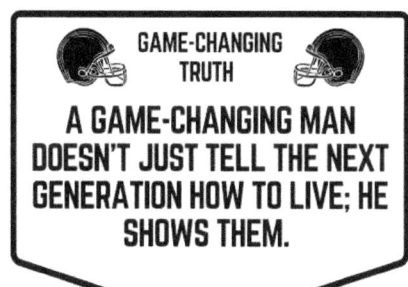

refuses to let culture have the final say. He intentionally steps into the lives of young men, offering his time, wisdom, prayers, and presence. He shows them what it looks like to be bold for Christ in a world that pulls them in every direction.

Building up the next generation takes sacrifice. It means giving up some comfort, rearranging your schedule, and choosing patience when mistakes are made. But the reward is eternal—every hour invested, every prayer prayed, every truth spoken—God multiplies.

Your mentorship may shape the pastor who preaches to thousands, the father who raises godly children, or the leader who transforms his community. The legacy of a game-changing man of God is not just what he accomplishes, but who he equips to carry the mission forward.

We don't need to rack up accomplishments; we need to rack up successors who can outdo us.

We can never claim true success in life until we have younger men under us put us out of commission spiritually. We achieve our greatest success in God's kingdom when we take off our helmets and become cheerleaders. When we realize this, God's kingdom will be unstoppable.

You see, it isn't about you or me; it is all about them! What they do in the kingdom. How they grow. What they accomplish. They will be our legacy. A game-changing man realizes this and builds a legend of game-changing men to take his place…and the kingdom grows.

As we come to a close, I would like us to join in one final prayer together.

Dear Heavenly Father,

My fellow teammates and I come humbly before You today. First, we ask You to forgive us for any times we have allowed pride to hold us back from investing ourselves in the next generation.

Father, we have chosen to become game-changing men. Please help us to be worthy mentors to the future generation. Move mightily in us and through us as we all work together to encourage the younger generation to not only get in the game, but to win! In Jesus' Name, Amen!

GROUP STUDY QUESTIONS:

1. Which Biblical example of mentorship inspires you the most, and why?
2. How can we overcome the fear of being replaced when mentoring younger men?
3. In what ways can you model Christlike behavior rather than just giving advice?
4. How can you celebrate and encourage the successes of younger men around you?
5. How can you counter the influence of culture and social media in the lives of the next generation?
6. What steps can you take to leave a lasting legacy by raising up game-changing men of God?
7. After reading this chapter, what is one thing you will put into practice or one thing you will change in your life?
8. How can we, as a group, help you do this?

WORKBOOK

WORKBOOK

CHAPTER ONE

Write your definition of *Game Changer*:

Write your plan for how you will approach this study, i.e., what day/time you will do the reading, etc., so you are prepared for your weekly men's group.

CONTRACT BETWEEN YOU AND GOD

(And your men's group)

Will you commit to:

Reading each chapter, including Scripture verses? Yes/No

Sincerely examine your heart using the questions at the end of each chapter? Yes/No

Openly discussing the chapter with the men in your group with honesty and vulnerability? Yes/No

I, _____, am committed to getting up off the mat and becoming an unbreakable man living a victorious life. I affirm this decision with my signature.

_____

    (Sign)   (Date)

WORKBOOK

CHAPTER TWO

KEY VERSE

The Lord sees not as man sees: man looks on the outward appearance, but the Lord looks on the heart. -1 Samuel 16:7 (ESV)

REFLECTION

NFL scouts misjudged J.J. Watt, and even David's own father overlooked him.

If someone wrote a *"scouting report"* on you, what strengths would they list?

What weaknesses or doubts do you think they'd highlight?

Which part of that *"report"* do you secretly fear might be true?

Write a few honest notes.

GAME CHANGERS

LIES VS. TRUTH

Below are some common lies men hear. Circle the ones you've believed, then write the truth from God's Word next to it.

Lie: *"You're worthless."*
Truth: Psalm 139:14 – ***I am fearfully and wonderfully made.***

Lie: *"You'll never amount to anything."*
Truth: Jeremiah 29:11 – ***God has plans to prosper me.***

Lie: *"You're weak."*
Truth: 2 Corinthians 12:9 – ***God's power is made perfect in my weakness.***

Lie: *"You're a failure."*
Truth: Romans 8:37 – ***I am more than a conqueror.***

Assignment: Write one or two lies you've carried that aren't on this list. Then find a verse that speaks the truth over it.

DAVID'S EXAMPLE

David faced harsh words from:

- Goliath (mocking)
- Nabal (disrespect)
- Shimei (curses)

Question:

Which of those moments feels most like your life right now?

How do you usually respond when criticized, mocked, or dismissed? (Circle one: fight back | shut down | prove them wrong | run to God)

How do you want to respond moving forward?

GAME CHANGER CHALLENGE

Write your own *"Declaration of Truth"* based on God's Word.
Example:
"I am chosen by God. I am not defined by others' words but by His Word. I am strong, loved, and equipped to live out His purpose for me."

This week's challenge:

- Read your declaration every morning.

- Speak it out loud the moment negative words or old lies creep in.

- At the end of the week, journal how it changed your confidence and mindset.

CHAPTER THREE

KEY VERSE

The integrity of the upright guides them, but the unfaithful are destroyed by their duplicity. -Proverbs 11:3 (NIV)

REFLECTION

Integrity is consistency between your private life and your public life. Joseph lived it everywhere: in slavery, in prison, and in the palace.

Questions:

When you hear of Christian leaders falling into scandal, how does it affect your faith?

Be honest: where are you most tempted to *"live two lives"*? (work, online, hidden habits, relationships)

What would change if the people closest to you saw every part of your life without filters?

Write out a few honest thoughts.

GAME CHANGERS

LIES VS. TRUTH

Men often justify compromise with lies. Below are some Joseph might have believed, and the truths he lived by.

Lie: *"No one will ever know."*
Truth: Luke 8:17 – **Nothing hidden will not be disclosed.**

Lie: *"I deserve this because I've suffered."*
Truth: Romans 12:21 – **Do not be overcome by evil, but overcome evil with good.**

Lie: *"I can bend my morals at work. It's just business."*
Truth: Colossians 3:23 – **Work heartily, as for the Lord and not for men.**

Lie: *"Power gives me special privileges."*
Truth: Proverbs 16:18 – **Pride goes before destruction.**

Assignment: Write down one lie you've told yourself in a tough season. Then find and record a verse that replaces it with God's truth.

JOSEPH'S EXAMPLE

Joseph showed integrity in five areas:

- Work (Potiphar's house, prison, Pharaoh's palace)
- Sexual temptation (Mrs. Potiphar)
- Victimhood (falsely accused and imprisoned)
- Power (leading Egypt during famine)
- Relationships (forgiving his brothers)

Questions:

Which of these five areas is your greatest challenge right now?

Which one do you feel strongest in?

What would it look like for you to *"Joseph-up"* in your weak spot?

GAME CHANGER CHALLENGE

Write a personal Integrity Statement that applies to your life today. Example:

"No matter where I am—home, work, or in private—I will be the same man. I choose honesty, purity, and faithfulness. My integrity is not for sale."

This week's challenge:

- Share your Integrity Statement with one trusted brother in Christ.
- Ask him to check in with you once this week to see if you're living it out.

CHAPTER FOUR

KEY VERSE

And who knows whether you have not come to the kingdom for such a time as this? -Esther 4:14 (ESV)

REFLECTION

Mordecai wasn't a king, prophet, or warrior. He was just a man of faith who took responsibility for his niece and spoke courage into her life. His encouragement helped Esther step into her destiny.

Who has spoken life-giving words into you, like Mordecai did for Esther? How did it change you?

Think about the women closest to you (wife, daughter, sister, friend, coworker). How do you usually respond when they step into leadership, success, or influence?

Be honest: do you see yourself more often cheering women on, or holding back? Why?

LIES VS. TRUTH

Lie: *"Men need to control, silence, or compete with women."*

Truth: God calls men and women to work side by side as co-laborers in His kingdom (Galatians 3:28).

Lie: *"If a woman succeeds, it threatens me."*

Truth: A game-changing man celebrates and supports the women around him because their victories advance God's purposes (Proverbs 31:29-31).

Write one area where you may have believed a lie, and replace it with God's truth.

BIBLICAL EXAMPLE

Mordecai saw God's calling on Esther's life and boldly told her, *"You can do this. You must do this."* Then he backed up his words with action by fasting, praying, and mobilizing others to support her.

What stands out to you most about Mordecai's example?

How does it challenge your own attitude toward the women God has placed in your life?

Where do you need to move from silence or passivity to active encouragement and support?

GAME CHANGER CHALLENGE

This week, choose one woman in your life to intentionally encourage. It could be affirming your wife's gifting, praising your daughter's courage, or thanking a female coworker for her leadership. Write out your encouragement before you give it, so your words are intentional.

CHAPTER FIVE

KEY VERSE

Always be prepared to give an answer to everyone who asks you to give the reason for the hope that you have. But do this with gentleness and respect. -1 Peter 3:15 (NIV)

REFLECTION

Charlie Kirk and Paul both remind us that truth can be explained clearly and confidently when we actually understand it. You can't share what you don't know.

Be honest: how confident do you feel explaining your faith to someone with hard questions? (circle one: very confident | somewhat confident | not confident at all)

Think about your own kids, friends, or coworkers: what is one faith question you hope they never ask you—because you don't know how to answer it?

How would your influence grow if you had a clear, Biblical answer?

Write out your thoughts.

LIES VS. TRUTH

Lie: *"I don't need to know theology—it's only for pastors."*
Truth: Deuteronomy 6:7 – Teach God's Word diligently to your children.

Lie: *"If I just share my testimony, that's enough."*
Truth: Acts 17 – Paul reasoned daily, explaining the Gospel with logic and clarity.

Lie: *"False teaching isn't that big of a deal."*
Truth: 1 Timothy 4:1 – ***In later times some will abandon the faith and follow deceiving spirits.***

Assignment: Write one lie you've believed about studying theology/apologetics and replace it with God's truth.

BIBLICAL EXAMPLE

Paul modeled how to adapt the Gospel message depending on his audience:

- To Jews, he quoted Scripture.
- To Greeks, he quoted poets.
- To farmers, he talked about rain and harvests.

Which example do you connect with most? Why?

How can you start learning enough theology to adjust your answers for different people you talk to?

What's one practical step you could take this week to strengthen your foundation?

GAME CHANGER CHALLENGE

This week, choose one resource from the list in the chapter (book, video, class, or study). Commit to engaging with it—read one chapter, watch one video, or start one course.

Write down what you will do, and when:

At the end of the week, share one new truth you learned with someone else (your spouse, a friend, or your kids).

WORKBOOK

CHAPTER SIX

KEY VERSE

Two are better than one, because they have a good return for their labor: If either of them falls down, one can help the other up. But pity anyone who falls and has no one to help them up. -Ecclesiastes 4:9–10 (NIV)

REFLECTION

We all want to be the quarterback under the lights, but even the best athletes need a hidden support team—stretching, taping, healing, and carrying their load. Silas was that kind of man for Paul.

Who has been a *"Silas"* in your life—someone who supported, encouraged, or carried you in a season when you were struggling?

Have you ever had a *"Mark"* experience—someone who quit on you when you needed them most? How did that affect you?

Be honest: do you usually see yourself more as the *"Paul"* (leading in front) or the *"Silas"* (faithful support behind the scenes)? Why?

GAME CHANGERS

LIES VS. TRUTH

Lie: *"If I'm not in front, I don't matter."*
Truth: 1 Corinthians 12:22 – The parts of the body that seem weaker are indispensable.

Lie: *"Supporting is less important than leading."*
Truth: Philippians 2:3 – ***In humility, value others above yourselves.***

Lie: *"Leaders don't need my encouragement or prayer."*
Truth: Hebrews 13:17 – Leaders keep watch over you as those who must give an account. Pray for them.

Assignment: Write down the name of one leader in your life (pastor, mentor, boss, father). Next to it, list one way you can actively support them this week.

SILAS'S EXAMPLE

Silas showed us four ways to be a game-changing man:

- He prayed with Paul in the midnight hour.
- He encouraged Paul in lonely, difficult times.
- He supported Paul when others criticized.
- He carried the load so Paul could focus on the mission.

Questions:

Which of these four comes easiest for you—praying, encouraging, supporting, or carrying the load?

Which one do you tend to neglect?

What would it look like to practice that area more intentionally this week?

GAME CHANGER CHALLENGE

Choose one leader in your life this week and commit to being a Silas to them:

- Pray for them daily.
- Send them an encouraging text or phone call.
- Publicly defend their reputation if you hear criticism.
- Volunteer to take one burden off their plate.

Write down the specific action you will take:

CHAPTER SEVEN

KEY VERSE

Have I not commanded you? Be strong and courageous. Do not be afraid; do not be discouraged, for the Lord your God will be with you wherever you go. -Joshua 1:9 (NIV)

REFLECTION

Nathan faced the most powerful man in Israel and risked everything by speaking the truth. He could have stayed quiet, but silence would have been deadly.

When have you chosen silence instead of speaking truth—and what was the result?

What fears usually keep you from speaking up (fear of rejection, fear of losing a relationship, fear of looking foolish, fear of conflict)?

Imagine you were Nathan, standing before David. What emotions would you feel in that moment?

LIES VS. TRUTH

Lie: *"Silence is safer. If I keep quiet, things won't get worse."*

Truth: Ezekiel 33:8 – **If I say to the wicked, 'You wicked person, you will surely die,' and you do not speak out… I will hold you accountable for their blood.**

Lie: *"Someone else will speak up. It's not my place."*

Truth: Esther 4:14 – **Who knows but that you have come to your royal position for such a time as this?**

Lie: *"Speaking the truth will cost me too much."*

Truth: Matthew 10:32 – **Whoever acknowledges me before others, I will also acknowledge before my Father in heaven.**

Assignment: Write down one area (home, work, friendships, church, culture) where you've been tempted to stay silent. Next to it, write one truth God is calling you to stand on this week.

NATHAN'S EXAMPLE

Nathan confronted David's sin with courage, not knowing if he would live to see another day.

What would have happened to Israel if Nathan had stayed silent?

How did David respond when Nathan finally spoke?

How can you balance truth with compassion when confronting someone you love?

GAME CHANGER CHALLENGE

This week, identify one person in your circle who needs truth spoken into their life. Do it prayerfully, gently, but firmly.

- If it's a friend drifting into sin—speak truth in love.
- If it's at work—instead of laughing along, take a stand.
- If it's in your family—start the hard conversation.

Write your *"Nathan moment"* for this week:

CHAPTER EIGHT

KEY VERSE

But Zacchaeus stood up and said to the Lord, "Look, Lord! Here and now I give half of my possessions to the poor, and if I have cheated anybody out of anything, I will pay back four times the amount." -Luke 19:8 (NIV)

REFLECTION

Every man has regrets—words we wish we could take back, choices that hurt people we love, seasons where selfishness left scars. The truth is, you can't rewrite the past, but you can change the future. Zacchaeus shows us that repentance isn't just feeling sorry—it's taking action to make things right.

What is one regret that still weighs on your heart?

How have your choices affected your family, friends, or children?

When you think about apologizing or making amends, what fears or excuses hold you back?

If someone hurt you deeply, what would you want them to do to rebuild trust?

GAME CHANGERS

LIES VS. TRUTH

Lie: *"If God forgives me, I don't need to apologize to people."*
Truth: Matthew 5:23–24 – **First be reconciled to your brother, then come and offer your gift.**

Lie: *"It's too late—I've messed up too much to ever make it right."*
Truth: Joel 2:25 – **I will restore to you the years that the locusts have eaten.**

Lie: *"An apology makes me look weak."*
Truth: James 4:10 – **Humble yourselves before the Lord, and He will lift you up.**

Assignment: Write down the name of one person you have hurt. Next to it, write the first step you could take toward making it right.

ZACCHAEUS'S EXAMPLE

Zacchaeus modeled true repentance by:

- Running to meet Jesus with urgency.
- Humbly welcoming Him into his home.
- Publicly confessing his sin.
- Going above and beyond to repay those he had wronged.

Questions:

Which part of Zacchaeus's response challenges you the most—urgency, humility, confession, or restitution?

In what specific area of your life do you need to *"pay back"* those you've hurt—not necessarily with money, but with love, consistency, and honesty?

What would change in your family if you lived out repentance as boldly as Zacchaeus?

GAME CHANGER CHALLENGE

This week, take one concrete step to rebuild a broken relationship:

- Admit your wrongs without excuses.
- Ask sincerely for forgiveness.
- Begin proving your repentance through consistency—showing up, keeping your word, choosing love over selfishness.

Write down your specific action step for this week:

CHAPTER NINE

KEY VERSE

I have filled him with the Spirit of God, with wisdom, with understanding, with knowledge and with all kinds of skills—to make artistic designs for work in gold, silver and bronze, to cut and set stones, to work in wood, and to engage in all kinds of crafts. -Exodus 31:3–5 (NIV)

REFLECTION

It's easy to think that only the men in the spotlight—pastors, preachers, leaders—are the ones truly making a difference for God's kingdom. But the Bible tells us about Bezalel, a man chosen and empowered by God not to preach or lead an army, but to build. His craftsmanship created the tabernacle, the place where God's presence would dwell among His people.

Behind-the-scenes men like Bezalel are just as game-changing as the warriors or prophets. Your skills—whether building, organizing, fixing, leading teams, or solving problems—can reflect the excellence of God when offered to Him.

What talents or skills has God uniquely given you?

Do you tend to downplay your gifts because they aren't *"in the spotlight"*?

GAME CHANGERS

In what ways have you used your skills to serve yourself instead of serving God?

How could your work (job, hobbies, or everyday tasks) become a reflection of God's excellence this week?

LIES VS. TRUTH

Lie: *"My skills don't matter as much as preaching, teaching, or leading."*
Truth: 1 Corinthians 12:18 – **God has placed the parts in the body, every one of them, just as He wanted them to be.**

Lie: *"Excellence isn't worth the effort—'good enough' will do."*
Truth: Colossians 3:23 – **Whatever you do, work at it with all your heart, as working for the Lord, not for human masters.**

Lie: *"What I do behind the scenes doesn't really count for eternity."*
Truth: Matthew 6:4 – **Your Father, who sees what is done in secret, will reward you.**

Assignment: Write down one skill or talent God has given you. Then write one way you can use it this week to bless others or strengthen the church.

BEZALEL'S EXAMPLE

Bezalel shows us that Spirit-filled excellence matters. He:

- Was filled with the Spirit of God to create and build.
- Used his skills with precision and care, reflecting God's holiness.
- Served God's purposes rather than his own fame.
- Built something that made worship possible for God's people.

Questions:

Which part of Bezalel's example challenges you most—being Spirit-filled, pursuing excellence, serving without recognition, or building for others?

What would change if you began to see your daily work as holy and Spirit-directed?

How might God be calling you to raise the standard from *"good enough"* to *"excellent"* in your current responsibilities?

GAME CHANGER CHALLENGE

This week, don't bury your gift—use it. Take one of your God-given abilities and intentionally offer it back to Him by:

- Serving your church in a practical way (maintenance, hospitality, technology, etc.).
- Bringing excellence to a task at work or home that you'd normally rush through.
- Offering your skills to someone in need, expecting nothing in return.

Write down the specific action you will take this week to use your gifts for God's glory:

CHAPTER TEN

KEY VERSE

Search me, God, and know my heart; test me and know my anxious thoughts. See if there is any offensive way in me, and lead me in the way everlasting. -Psalm 139:23-24 (NIV)

REFLECTION

It's easy to read Joshua's story with hindsight and think, *"What's the problem? God already promised him victory!"* But Joshua didn't know the end of the story. He only knew that Moses was gone, he was now responsible for leading an entire nation, and their first battle was against Jericho—a fortified city with walls 30 feet high and 20 feet thick.

Joshua wasn't told how God would deliver. He had to trust, obey, and move forward with courage. Like Joshua, we fight battles today—not with swords, but with sin, temptation, and spiritual strongholds. The call is still the same: Be strong and courageous.

What *"Jericho walls"* are you facing right now—obstacles that look too big to overcome?

When has fear or discouragement kept you from obeying God?

What does it look like for you to step into courage even when you don't know the outcome?

LIES VS. TRUTH

Lie: *"I'll never defeat this sin or struggle—it's too strong."*
Truth: Philippians 4:13 – **I can do all things through Christ who strengthens me.**

Lie: *"Admitting I have a problem makes me weak."*
Truth: James 5:16 – **Confess your sins to each other and pray for each other so that you may be healed.**

Lie: *"If I ignore it, it will eventually go away."*
Truth: John 8:32 – **Then you will know the truth, and the truth will set you free.**

Assignment: Write down one area of your life where you need to pray Psalm 139:23–24 (**"Search me, O God"**). Be specific and ask the Holy Spirit to reveal the root of the issue.

JOSHUA'S EXAMPLE

Joshua shows us that courage doesn't mean having no fear—it means obeying God in spite of fear. His example teaches us:

- He accepted the responsibility God gave him, even when it felt overwhelming.
- He trusted God's presence without knowing the outcome.
- He faced intimidating enemies and impossible walls with faith.
- He led the people into victory by obeying God's direction step by step.

Questions:

Which of Joshua's steps challenges you the most—accepting responsibility, trusting God's presence, facing enemies, or obeying step by step?

How does your *"battlefield"* today (sin, addiction, fear, or temptation) require courage like Joshua's battlefield did?

What practical step can you take this week to walk in obedience even when you feel fear?

GAME CHANGER CHALLENGE

This week, choose one area where fear, sin, or discouragement has kept you from moving forward.

Commit to:

- Praying Psalm 139:23–24 sincerely, asking God to reveal hidden sin or strongholds.

- Taking one courageous action step toward freedom (confession, accountability, counseling, joining a support group, etc.).

- Refusing to settle for *"good enough"* or partial victory—asking God for full freedom.

Write down the courageous step you will take this week:

CHAPTER ELEVEN

KEY VERSE

A man who has friends must himself be friendly, but there is a friend who sticks closer than a brother. -Proverbs 18:24 (NKJV)

REFLECTION

Who are your closest friends right now? How many would you say truly *"know"* you—your struggles, victories, and heart?

Do you tend to keep friendships surface-level (based mostly on activities) or do you go deeper and talk about real life?

Think about Jonathan's loyalty to David. Would your friends describe you as that loyal? Why or why not?

Have you ever pulled back from celebrating someone else's success because of jealousy? What did that reveal about your heart?

When was the last time you encouraged or strengthened a friend *"in the Lord"* the way Jonathan did for David?

LIES VS. TRUTH

Lie #1: *"Real men don't need close friends. Independence is strength."*

Truth: Even Jesus surrounded Himself with close friends (Peter, James, John) and poured into the Twelve. Real strength comes from brotherhood.

Lie #2: *"Friendships are only about fun or shared activities."*

Truth: Biblical friendship means loyalty, accountability, encouragement, and truth-speaking (Proverbs 27:6).

Lie #3: *"If I open up, I'll look weak."*

Truth: Vulnerability builds trust and deepens friendship. Jonathan and David shared openly, even when their lives were at risk (1 Samuel 20).

Write down reasons you struggle being a good friend, then write down steps to overcome.

JONATHAN'S EXAMPLE

Jonathan risked his position, his safety, and even his relationship with his father to protect David. He celebrated David's victories instead of being jealous, spoke truth when it was dangerous, and strengthened David's faith when he was weary.

Proverbs 18:24 (NKJV): *"A man who has friends must himself be friendly, but there is a friend who sticks closer than a brother."*

Questions:

Am I the kind of friend who celebrates others' successes, even when it costs me something?

Do I speak truth and stand by what's right, even when it could hurt my reputation or relationships?

How can I strengthen and encourage my friends' faith when they're feeling weary or discouraged?

GAME CHANGER CHALLENGE

This week, take one intentional step toward building or deepening a friendship:

- Call or text a friend and ask how he's really doing. Don't settle for *"I'm fine."*

- Share one personal struggle with a trusted friend and invite accountability.

- Celebrate a friend's win (work, family, faith, or personal growth) without comparison.

- Make a plan to regularly connect with one or two brothers in Christ—coffee, prayer, or just time together.

Remember: friendships don't just happen—they're built. Be the kind of friend you want others to be for you.

CHAPTER TWELVE

KEY VERSE

And the things you have heard me say in the presence of many witnesses entrust to reliable people who will also be qualified to teach others. -2 Timothy 2:2 (NIV)

REFLECTION

Just like in dynasty fantasy football, where you build for the future and pass on strength to the next generation, God calls men to think beyond their own lifetime. We are not just playing for today—we're investing in the team that comes after us.

Who mentored you in your faith? What impact did their influence have on your life?

Have you ever held back from mentoring someone because of insecurity or fear of being *"replaced"*?

Do you see yourself more as a *"player"* right now (in the game) or a *"coach"* (equipping others)? Why?

How does the phrase *"My ceiling is the next generation's floor"* challenge your perspective on legacy?

LIES VS. TRUTH

Lie: *"I need to protect my position. If I help others, they'll outshine me."*
Truth: John 3:30 – **He must become greater; I must become less.**

Lie: *"Mentorship is optional. I just need to focus on my own walk with God."*
Truth: Matthew 28:19 – **Go and make disciples of all nations…** Mentorship is discipleship—it's a command.

Lie: *"Young men don't want guidance."*
Truth: Proverbs 9:9 – **Instruct the wise and they will be wiser still; teach the righteous and they will add to their learning.**

Assignment: Write down one younger man you know who could use encouragement, prayer, or guidance. What's one specific step you could take this week to invest in him?

BIBLICAL EXAMPLE

The Bible is full of dynasty builders:

- Moses mentored Joshua.
- Elijah mentored Elisha.
- Paul mentored Timothy and Titus.
- Jesus mentored the Twelve.

Each of these men understood the power of passing the torch. Their influence extended far beyond their own lives because they raised up leaders who carried the mission further.

Questions:

Which Biblical mentoring relationship inspires you most, and why?

Who do you see in your life that you could intentionally begin to mentor?

What are one or two lessons God has taught you that you could pass on to someone younger?

GAME CHANGER CHALLENGE

This week, take one practical step to invest in the next generation:

- Share a story with a younger man about a lesson you learned the hard way.
- Invite someone younger to join you for coffee or lunch and just listen.
- Commit to praying daily for one young man in your life.
- Celebrate and encourage one *"win"* in a younger man's life.

Write down the step you'll take: _____

BIBLIOGRAPHY

Chapter 1

1. Gosselin, Rick . "*Draft Review: J.J. Watt Overcame the Rap on Wisconsin Defensive Linemen.*" Rickgosselin.com, 22 Jul. 2022, rickgosselin.com/draft-review-j-j-watt/. Accessed 30 Sept. 2025.

Chapter 3

1. CCM Magazine Staff. "*Michael Tait Breaks Silence: My Confession.*" Ccmmagazine.com, 10 Jun. 2025, www.ccmmagazine.com/news/michael-tait-breaks-silence-my-confession/. Accessed 30 Sept. 2025.

2. "*Gutfeld!.*" *Gutfeld!,* hosted by Greg Gutfeld, Fox News, 12 Sept. 2025. Hulu, www.hulu.com

3. "*Integrity.*" *Cambridge Dictionary,* Cambridge University Press and Assessment, 2025, https://dictionary.cambridge.org/dictionary/english/integrity.

Chapter 4

1. *Christmas at Dollywood.* Directed by Michael Robison, performances by Danica McKellar and Niall Matter, Dollywood Christmas Productions, Two 4 The Money Media, Emerald Bay Entertainment, 2019.

2. *Beverly Hills Ninja.* Directed by Dennis Dugan , performances by Chris Farley and Nicholette Sheridan, TriStar Pictures, Motion Pictures Corporation of America, 1997.

3. *"After Hours." Blue Bloods*, created by Robin Green and Mitchell Burgess, season #1, episode 10, Panda Productions, Paw in Your Face Productions, CBS Productions, 2010.

4. *"The Wedding." The Middle*, created by Eileen Heisler, DeAnn Heline, season #3, episode 23, Blackie and Blondie Productions, Warner Bros. Television, 2012.

5. "Marcus Aurelius Quotes." BrainyQuote.com. BrainyMedia Inc, 2025. 1 October 2025. https://www.brainyquote.com/quotes/marcus_aurelius_132163

6. *The Dave Ramsey Show*. "Dave talks on The Ramsey Show about a funny encounter with an electronics salesman trying to sell him an extended warranty." Facebook, 31 Mar. 2025, https://www.facebook.com/watch/?v=1152322573358033.

7. *"Hepatitis." M.A.S.H*, created by Larry Gelbart, season #5, episode 19, 20th Century Fox Television, 1977.

Chapter 5

1. *"Hebrew/Greek Keyword Study: "dialegomai" (G1363)." BibleGateway.com*, Zondervan, https://www.biblegateway.com/passage/?search=Acts%2017%3A16-17&version=NIV

2. Barker, Kenneth L. And John R Kohlenberger III. *Zondervan NIV Bible Commentary Vol 2: New Testament.* Grand Rapids, Mi: Zondervan Publishing House, 1994, Pg 476.

3. *"Creighton Abrams Quotes."* BrainyQuote.com. BrainyMedia Inc, 2025. 1 October 2025. https://www.brainyquote.com/quotes/creighton_abrams_207381

Chapter 8

1. *"Love Eventually."* Chesapeake Shores, created by John Tinker and Nancey Silvers, season #3, episode 5, Chesapeake Shores Productions Inc., 2018.

Chapter 10

1. J. Wesley Adams, *Introduction to Joshua, Fire Bible: English Standard Version,* (Peabody, MA: Henderickson Publishers Marketing, LLC, 2014), Pg 314.

2. Donald C Stamps, *Study Notes on Joshua 6:1, Fire Bible: English Standard Version,* (Peabody, MA: Hendrickson Publishers Marketing, LLC, 2014), Pg 322.

3. Frangipane, Francis. *The Three Battlegrounds.* Arrow Publications, 1989. pp. 35-39.

Chapter 11

1. *The Waterboy.* Directed by Frank Coraci, performances by Adam Sandler and Kathy Bates , Touchstone Pictures, Jack Giarraputo Productions, Robert Simonds Productions, 1998.

2. Cox, *Daniel A.* "Men's Social Circles Are Shrinking." Survey Center on American Life, 29 Jun. 2021, www.americansurveycenter.org/why-mens-social-circles-are-shrinking/. Accessed 25 Sept. 2025.

3. Uncredited Author. *"Movember."* Survey Center on American Life, 31 Oct. 2018, uk.movember.com/story/view/id/11740/men-s-health-survey?). Accessed 25 Sept. 2025.

Chapter 12

1. Klis, Mike (@mikeklis9news). *"Dobbins on mentoring RJ Harvey: "Whenever I came in as a rookie with the Baltimore Ravens I had a Heisman Trophy winner, a guy who was well-established in Mark*

Ingram. And no matter what, he would always give what was right by me. I saw that and it meant ... Mark and I are still best friends today. He was a great mentor, a great veteran. He was teaching me things that were helping me get better as a football player. That meant the world to me because at the end of the day we're all chasing a dream. "So now it's my job to help the young man get to where he needs to go because eventually I'm going to retire and when I retire I want to look back and say I really helped that kid. If he's still playing and I'm retired, I want to look and say, 'I taught him that. I told him to do that.' It's kind of like having a little brother. And it helps us win games." Twitter, 1 Sept. 2025, 10:39 a.m., https://x.com/mikeklis9news/status/1969048636266090829?s=10.

Also Available

WITH THE FIRST PICK OF THE DRAFT
GOD CHOOSES YOU!
Put your faith into action with this year-long Bible reading plan designed to help you become a Game Changing Man of God!

VISIT WWW.MANTOURMINISTRIES.COM//BIBLEPLAN

ALSO AVAILABLE FROM MANTOUR MINISTRIES:

**Available in print and digital formats.
Visit www.mantourministries.com
for more information.**

We can't do it alone.
Your partnership enables us to:

-Host Mantour Conferences

Last year, over 1,100 men from over 110 churches attended their local Mantour Conference.

We were also blessed to have over 70 men from Teen Challenge Centers, half-way houses, and homeless shelters attend for FREE as our guests.

In July, we held a Free Mantour Conference at Teen Challenge Rehrersburg.

-Outreach

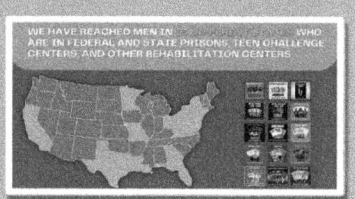

Each year, Mantour Ministries invites men from Teen Challenge Centers, halfway houses, and homeless shelters to attend Mantour Conferences as our guests.

The Mantour Challenge offering also allows us to donate books and Bible plans to prisons and Teen Challenge Centers, reaching men in 15 states.

-Produce Men's Ministry Resources

Each year, Jamie writes a new book to go with the Mantour Conference theme.

Because we believe men need to be in God's Word, we create a Daily Bible Reading Plan just for men. This resource is available as a book or for free via email. It is also featured on the Penndel Men's Ministry page.

We created the "Hitting Below the Belt" booklet to help men overcome pornography and sexual sin.

Each week, we provide encouragement to men on social media using video teaching and written encouragement.

JOIN OUR FINANCIAL SUPPORT TEAM TODAY AND HELP US REACH MORE MEN WITH THE GOSPEL!
HTTPS://WWW.MANTOURMINISTRIES.COM/PARTNER

Jamie loves to speak to men and is available to speak at your next men's event. Jamie combines humor and his personal testimony to engage and challenge men to grow in their walk with God. He uses his testimony of overcoming abuse and dealing with his physical and emotional issues growing up to encourage men that no matter what their background or where they have come from in life, they can grow into mighty men in God's kingdom.

"Years ago, while I was attending the University of Valley Forge, God gave me a deep desire to minister to men. My calling is to help men learn what it means to be a godly man and how to develop a deep, personal relationship with their heavenly Father. We strive to challenge and encourage men to reach their full potential in God's kingdom."

If you are interested in having Jamie at your next men's event as a speaker or workshop leader, or if you are interested in having him come share with your church, contact him by visiting www.mantourministries.com/invitejamie. He is also available to speak for one or multiple weeks on the theme of his books.

www.ingramcontent.com/pod-product-compliance
Lightning Source LLC
Chambersburg PA
CBHW050903160426
43194CB00011B/2262